TRACING Y
DOCKER
ANCESTORS

FAMILY HISTORY FROM PEN & SWORD

TRACING YOUR DOCKER ANCESTORS

A Guide for Family Historians

Alex Ombler

Pen & Sword
FAMILY HISTORY

First published in Great Britain in 2019
PEN & SWORD FAMILY HISTORY
an imprint of
Pen & Sword Books Ltd
Yorkshire — Philaddelphia

ISBN 978 1 52674 404 3

A CIP catalogue record for this book is
available from the British Library.

Typeset in Palatino and Optima by CHIC GRAPHICS

Printed and bound in England by TJ International Ltd, Padstow, Cornwall

Pen & Sword Books Ltd incorporates the imprints of Pen & Sword
Airworld, Archaeology, Atlas, Aviation, Battleground, Discovery, Family
History, Fiction, History, Maritime, Military, Military Classics, Politics,
Select, Social History, True Crime, Frontline Books, Leo Cooper,
Remember When, Seaforth Publishing, The Praetorian Press,
Wharncliffe Local History, Wharncliffe Transport,
Wharncliffe True Crime and White Owl.

For a complete list of Pen & Sword titles please contact

PEN & SWORD BOOKS LTD
47 Church Street, Barnsley, South Yorkshire, S70 2AS, England
E-mail: enquiries@pen-and-sword.co.uk
Website: www.pen-and-sword.co.uk
or
PEN & SWORD BOOKS LTD
1950 Lawrence Rd., Havertown, PA 19083, USA
E-mail: Uspen-and-sword@casematepublishers.com
Website: www.penandswordbooks.com

CONTENTS

INTRODUCTION

The British dock labour force was one of the largest and most important working groups in the country during the nineteenth and twentieth centuries. In 1921 some 125,000 dockers were employed across the country's numerous ports, where millions of tons of seaborne cargo were handled annually. Amongst the imported goods unloaded by the dockers were foodstuffs which fed the nation, whilst raw materials such as timber, cotton, wool and metal ores arrived on the docks for processing across various industries. The export cargos loaded by dock workers, mainly manufactures and coal, were sold overseas and brought wealth to the nation. In addition, the dockers' contribution to trade unionism was a vital step in the creation of the modern labour movement. Most notably the Great Dock Strike of 1889 galvanized other unskilled workers into collective action to gain improvements in pay and working conditions.

Despite being an essential cog in Britain's port transport system, the dockers remain a largely unknown group. Entry into dock work, which largely took place behind the dock wall, was virtually impossible for outsiders. Consequently the dockers' working practices, organization and culture were shrouded in mystery. This was often exploited by the media who regularly scapegoated the dockers and their industrial action for the economic ills of the day. The cargo-handling revolution in the 1960s caused many of the old docks, quays and sheds where the dockers worked to fall into disuse and dereliction. During the 1980s, many of these areas were redeveloped as luxury waterfront accommodation, retail and business centres, and leisure sites.

Dockers at work in gangs unloading a cargo of bananas c. 1937. Image courtesy of Maritime Museum: Hull Museums.

Today there is little trace in the landscape that the dockers ever existed.

The aim of this book is twofold. First, it provides a history of the dockers from their origins in the mid-nineteenth century to their decline and eventual disappearance by the late 1980s. This history provides a background to the personal experiences of those who worked on the docks. It must be noted that, although Britain's dockers as a whole were similar in character, the dock labour forces of each port had their own localized traditions, practices and terminology. As there is not space to deal with all of the nuances of dockland, the historical information in this book has been written with a general pattern of experience in mind. Second, the book identifies the types of records and artefacts that can give family historians an insight into the lives of the dockers. Furthermore, it provides a practical guide on where such sources can be found and how they can be accessed.

The first chapter is intended as a starting point and offers a guide on widely used family history sources. This will help establish a firm foundation of basic information including names, dates and places, upon which more specialized research can be built. The following Chapters 2 to 8 are thematic in nature and explore different aspects of dock life between c. 1840 and the 1960s. This includes the origins of the work force, the development of trade unionism on the docks, the daily working lives of the dockers, the tools they used, their culture and community outside of work, the role they played in both World Wars, and the Government's innovative attempts to improve their organization via the National Dock Labour Scheme. The final chapter deals with the technological developments in cargo-handling that emerged after the Second World War and the large-scale Government reforms in the port transport industry in response to such change. It also explores the how these reforms caused the decline and disappearance of the dockers' culture and traditions, which had endured for generations.

Chapter 1

GETTING STARTED: BASIC FAMILY HISTORY DOCUMENTS

When setting out to research family history it is generally advisable to start with known facts about your family and then work backwards, step by step. For example, if you know the details of your grandfather's birth then his birth or baptism certificate will give the names of his parents, so next you could look for their marriage and births or baptisms. It is essential to speak to family members, particularly older generations, and find out as much as possible. In addition, check any family records such as certificates, letters and photographs. Information that could be useful would be names, family relationships, dates, where people lived or which church they attended.

This chapter introduces several key types of document that can be used to build on basic known information. Most of these records are readily available in local archives or online with registration or relevant subscription to the family history websites www.ancestry.co.uk or www.findypast.co.uk and for Scotland at www.scotlandspeople.gov.uk. It is important to note that many archives and libraries subscribe to these and other sites and offer free public access.

Essential details such as names, dates and places can be gleaned from many of the documents outlined here. The final section of this chapter is a case study of a real dock worker, which shows how basic information can be used to build a profile of an ancestor.

Such a profile will provide a solid basis for the more specific docker-related research methods and materials that are discussed in the following chapters. Some of the documents mentioned in this chapter are also relevant to later parts of the book and will be referred back to at various points.

CIVIL REGISTRATION OF BIRTHS, MARRIAGES AND DEATHS

From 1 July 1837 births, marriages and deaths occurring in England and Wales have been officially recorded by civil authorities and certificates issued to those concerned. From the start, the country has been divided into registration districts each with its own Superintendent Registrar. Each registration district is divided into sub-districts. Birth, marriage and death certificates created by registration are held by, and can be purchased from, local register officers and online from the General Registry Office (GRO) www.gov.uk/order-copy-birth-death-marriage-certificate. For online copies of certificates it is advisable to obtain a reference number, which consists of a volume number and a page number. References for births and deaths can be found using the GRO's online indexes at www.gro.gov.uk/gro/content/certificates, this requires the creation of a free login. Alternatively, GRO references for births, deaths and marriages can be acquired from www.free bmd.org.uk.

PARISH REGISTERS

The parish registers of the Church of England record baptisms, marriages and burials and are therefore useful for tracing life events, particularly before the introduction of civil registration in 1837. The format of registers and the information they contain varies depending on their date. The early 'general' registers cover baptisms, marriages and burials usually with single line entries e.g. date then 'John son of William Smith baptised'. Separate printed marriage registers commenced in 1754, with a

2

more detailed version being introduced in 1837. Separate printed registers for baptisms and burials were used after 1812. Many parish registers have been deposited with local archives and record offices, but more recent registers may still be at the parish church. A large number of those held by local archives and record offices have been digitized and made available on Findmypast.

It is important to make note of ancestors who were Nonconformists. Nonconformists are those who belong to Protestant churches other than the Church of England; this includes Baptists, Congregationalists, Methodists, Presbyterians and Quakers. Many of these groups kept registers of births or baptisms and deaths or burials although some such as Baptists did not believe in the baptism of children. Marriages between 1754 and 1836 had to be conducted in an Anglican church, except for Jews and Quakers, and should be recorded in the parish registers. Marriages could take place in Nonconformist chapels from 1837 in the presence of a civil registrar who recorded the ceremony. Many early Nonconformist registers were passed to the Registrar General in 1840 and these are held at The National Archives in London, many of which are now available online with a relevant subscription to Ancestry.

Many Catholic registers remain in the custody of parish priests, so it is advisable to contact the relevant parish or diocese. Some Catholic registers housed in local archives have been digitized and indexed and are available online. Registers from the Diocese of Liverpool are on Ancestry, whilst others including those of Cheshire are on Findmypast. Catholic parish records from Ireland are outlined in detail in the following chapter.

CENSUS RETURNS

The first national census of England and Wales was taken in 1801 and one has been completed every ten years since then, except in 1941. Census returns are only available when they are over 100 years old. The national returns for 1801 to 1831 contain only statistical information. Thereafter returns record the name, age and occupation of residents in each household, and from 1851 details of place of birth, marital status and the relationship to the head of the household are included. Ages in the 1841 census tended to be rounded down to the nearest 5 years so that someone aged 27 could officially appear as 25. The censuses that are currently available were conducted on the following days:

1841, 6 June
1851, 30 March
1861, 7 April
1871, 2 April
1881, 3 April
1891, 5 April
1901, 31 March
1911, 2 April
1921, 19 June (this will be released in 2022)

Census records are arranged by district, then by parish and street. It sometimes can be difficult to compare one census year with another or to locate a particular property because house numbers are not always noted. The enumerator who collected the information also did not always follow the same route. In addition, some details may be inaccurate if people were unsure about their age or birthplace or if the enumerator recorded them incorrectly. Census returns were also taken every ten years in Scotland from 1841.

THE 1939 REGISTER
The 1939 register is an essential source of information for those looking to learn more about the family and community lives of their ancestors in England and Wales during the first half of the twentieth century (the register did not cover the civilian

populations of Scotland, Northern Ireland, the Channel Islands or the Isle of Man). It is particularly vital as the 1931 census, which would have been made publicly accessible in 2031, was destroyed during an air raid on London.

In December 1938 it was announced in the House of Commons that, in the event of war, a National Register was to be taken listing the personal details of civilians. The Register was to be a critical tool in coordinating the war effort at home and would be used primarily to issue identity cards and to organize rationing and conscription. On 5 September 1939, two days after the declaration of war, it was declared that National Registration Day would take place later that month. On 29 September more than 41 million people were issued with forms that recorded names, addresses, marital statuses, exact dates of birth, occupation and whether the individual was a member of the armed services or reserves. However, unlike a census it does not include place of birth. It must also be noted that those on active duty in the military were not included in the headcount, even if they were billeted in the household and were there on the night of the headcount. From 1948 the Register was also used as the National Health Service (NHS) Register and, as a result, deaths, marriages and other information were updated.

On 2 November 2015 the 1939 Register was released online by Findmypast in partnership with The National Archives and is available to view with a subscription at www.findmypast.co.uk/1939register. A version of the register is also available on Ancestry. The records of people born less than 100 years ago and not known to have died before 1991 are closed due to privacy laws. As more records become open as a result of the 100 year rule, more records will become available to search and view.

ELECTORAL REGISTERS AND POLL BOOKS
Historic electoral registers and poll books are widely accessible at local archives and record offices. Electoral registers list the

individuals entitled to vote at elections, which was originally based on a property qualification. All men over 21 were then given the right to vote in 1918 and this was extended to women over 21 in 1928. From 1832 annual registers were compiled, giving the names of electors and the property that qualified them to vote. There were, however no registers printed for 1916, 1917 or 1940–4 because of the World Wars. Entries within each register are arranged by polling district, parish and then by surname or occasionally by street and then surname in larger districts. Registers are usually arranged and listed according to the various electoral divisions, which often change several times in the past. The registers may be time consuming to check especially if you are unsure about the address and the years concerned. However, they are useful for confirming when a person lived at a specific address as well as providing a list of adults resident in a property, mainly in the twentieth century.

Poll books are lists of the names of voters and who they voted for, occasionally they also record the voter's residence, occupation and voting qualification. Secret ballots were introduced from 1872 which meant poll books were no longer produced. The proportion of the population entitled to vote before this date is, however, relatively small.

WILLS AND PROBATE

Wills can answer many important family history questions about family relationships, and about how people lived. Furthermore, it is possible to find names of family members, their relationships and details of everyday possessions. You may also find details of the debts that they owed at the time of their death. All wills contain: where the deceased lived, the name of the executor (person responsible for carrying out their wishes), the date of the will, witnesses, and chief beneficiaries. Before January 1858 a complicated network of probate courts existed to deal with the distribution of property following a person's death. The Principal

Probate Registry was established on 12 January 1858 and keeps a copy of every will proved in England or Wales after 1858, as well as copies of letters of administration. To search and purchase wills proved after 1858 visit www.gov.uk/wills-probate-inheritance/searching-for-probate-records. For wills proved in Scotland up to 1925 visit www.scotlandspeople.gov.uk/guides/wills-and-testaments and from 1925 onwards go to www.nrscotland.gov.uk/research/guides/wills-and-testaments.

NEWSPAPERS

Newspapers can be immensely useful as sources of information for family historians as they include notices of family events, obituaries and reports of court cases and coroners' inquests. Most local archives and libraries hold historic local newspapers, often on microfilm. Alternatively, many local newspapers that are still in existence have their own archives. A sizeable number of regional and national historic British newspapers have been digitized and are available online either free or with a subscription fee. Again, check local libraries, archives and record offices who may offer free public access to the following sites:

The British Newspaper Archive: www.britishnewspaper archive. co.uk and www.findmypast.co.uk. The British Newspaper Archive is provided jointly by the British Library and Findmypast and offers a vast collection of local, national and regional newspapers titles from across the UK and Ireland. Although the site is free to search online, to view content requires a monthly or yearly subscription or Pay As You Go on the British Newspaper Archive site. The collection is included in a Findmypast subscription and is free to view at the British Library's Reading Rooms at St Pancras and Boston Spa.

The Times Digital Archive: holds copies: www.thetimes.co.uk/archive/. The Times Archive holds fully searchable electronic copies of *The Times* from 1785–2012. Various subscription packages are offered, however, and many libraries offer free public access.

The Guardian **and** *Observer* **Digital Archive:** https://the guardian.newspapers.com/. This archive holds more than 1.2 million pages of the *Guardian* (1821–2003) and *Observer* (1791–1923) newspapers. There is information on past national affairs but also important milestones in the lives of some people, including birth and wedding announcements and obituaries. Searching and viewing requires payment, but subscriptions can be purchased for 24 hours or up to a year.

National Library of Scotland: www.nls.uk/collections/ newspapers. This digital collection includes items ranging from the earliest newspaper printed in Scotland to modern titles. The site features access to the British Newspaper Archive, which contains Scottish titles including the *Ayr Advertiser*, the *Glasgow Herald* and the *Stirling Observer*.

The Scotsman: http://archive.scotsman.com/. *The Scotsman* was a liberal weekly broadsheet that dates back to 1817. The site's searchable records go up to 1950. It is free to search, but viewing involves a charge. Subscription packages from two days to 12 months can be purchased.

Welsh Newspapers Online: http://newspapers.library.wales. This fully searchable website run by the National Library of Wales features over one million pages from newspaper titles up to 1910. It is free to search and view online.

Irish Newspaper Archives: www.Irishnewsarchive.com. This website contains millions of newspaper pages from all over Ireland (including Northern Ireland). It includes a useful digital map so that you can see which newspapers were published in which area. Searches are free but subscription, for one day, by month or by year, is needed to view content.

FAMILY PHOTOGRAPHS

Photographs of dock workers are unfortunately rare, but are an essential item that can tell us about ancestors on the docks. Most of the images in the handbooks, annual reports and other literature produced by port authorities are of port facilities and ships: any dock workers captured in these scenes are often incidental. Yet, photographs of dockers can be found elsewhere

A family photograph showing a group of dockers on a German ship, taken during the 1950s.

in personal, private and public collections. The first step for those trying to find photographs of their docker ancestors is to look through family photograph albums, particularly at images during and after the 1930s when amateur photography became popular. If no information is recorded on the reverse, such as the name(s) of people in the image, the date it was captured and the location where it was taken, it is important if possible to do so (preferably in a soft lead pencil) for future reference. In terms of identifying people in photographs, try speaking to older generations to see if they may recognize the subjects. Dating photographs is not always easy, but messages are hidden in clothes, hairstyles and objects. However, this can be difficult in the case of dockers as their tools and traditional working attire, which was often simple and consisted of a flat cap, changed little prior to modernization during the 1960s and the widespread introduction of safety equipment in the 1970s. When trying to establish the location of photographs taken of dockers at work, try noting any cargoes, tools or buildings, as particular goods and associated handling equipment were often associated with specific areas of a dock or port. Posting images on social media sites, especially on any local heritage or nostalgia pages can help provide information relating to names, dates and places.

Case Study: James William Senior, docker

This case study provides an example of how a simple timeline of events for docker ancestors can be built up using the basic family history documents outlined in this chapter: James William Senior's birth certificate shows that he was born on 24 October 1878 . According to parish records, his parents, William and Elizabeth, had James baptised shortly after his birth on 31 March 1878 at St. Mary's Church. The parish records for St. Mark's Church indicate that James, a 'labourer' aged 22 married Emily Cockerill also aged 22 on 31 March 1900. A year later the couple were recorded in the 1901 census as living at

---

no. 117 Lime Street in Hull. According to local history books and ordnance survey maps Lime Street was a cramped industrial area close to the River Hull, a short distance from the port's Victoria Dock where timber was handled. A decade later, the 1911 census shows James, a 'dock worker', and Emily were still living at the same '3 roomed' residence, but now had 5 children; Albert (aged 10), Martha (aged 8), James (aged 6), Florrie (aged 5) and Ernest (aged 3).

James' death certificate reveals that he died in 1944 towards the end of the Second World War. The 1939 Register indicates that his son, James, had followed his father into dock work as he was a 'Dock Transport Worker'. At

A family photograph of docker James William Senior (1878–1944).

that time James was living at Endyke Lane in the north west of the city where, according to local history books, new housing had been built during the interwar years.

Basic family history documents tells us much about the general pattern of James' life; his parents, birth, baptism, marriage, death, occupation and residence. There is, however, much we don't know about one of the main aspects of his life story, that is, his working life on the docks. When did he start work? Why did he work there? Was he involved in a trade union? Which one? What did he do at work? What were conditions like? Where did he go outside of work? The information and records discussed in the following chapters provide a guide that can lead to answers and help researchers learn more about different aspects of their ancestor's working lives as a docker.

Chapter 2

THE ORIGINS OF THE DOCK LABOUR FORCE

As long as there have been ships carrying cargoes on the seas and waterways there has been a need for labourers to move goods between ship and shore. One of the earliest recorded labourers of this type were the medieval 'creelers' of Beverley in East Yorkshire. Creelers carried goods from vessels berthed in the River Hull to the nearby market town of Beverley. Whilst cargo-handling labour existed even before the creelers, it was in the nineteenth century, during the great age of dock construction, when the occupation of the dock labourer or 'docker' was truly defined. The first part of this chapter outlines the development of British ports during these years and how this created a growing demand for a large labour force to discharge and load a wide variety of seaborne goods. The second part offers a guide to the records that can be used to learn more about the ancestral origins of the dockers.

THE GROWTH OF BRITISH PORTS, 1840–1914

Britain's large-scale industrialization during the nineteenth and early twentieth centuries stimulated the huge growth of the nation's global and coastwise seaborne trades. Imported goods were largely made up of bulk raw materials like iron, timber, cotton and wool. These were processed in the country's expanding industrial towns and cities, where growing urban

The medieval 'creelers' are one of the earliest recorded labour groups dedicated to the handling of waterborne cargoes between ship and shore. Photograph by Hannah Rice.

populations in turn created demand for other imports like foodstuffs including meat, grain, fruit, vegetables and dairy produce. The manufactures and goods produced in such places were the nation's main exports alongside coal from the coal fields around the country.

The growth of trade during this period had been enabled by the introduction and widespread use of steam engines. Steam-

14

powered ships were not reliant on wind and tide like the sailing vessels they increasingly replaced, whilst the railways could move goods between ships and inland areas far more efficiently than sailing vessels on the canals. This new transport technology needed new specialized port facilities. During the eighteenth and early nineteenth centuries commercial docks had been built at Liverpool, Hull, Leith and London, but these were too small for increasingly large steamships that needed ever-wider entrance locks. Furthermore, the older docks were situated in congested areas with only narrow lanes used by carts that were not spacious enough for the tracks, yards and sheds of the railways. From the middle of the nineteenth century various port authorities, including railway, canal, harbour and dock companies, constructed new docks and other facilities at both new and old port locations.

The larger ports were predominantly situated on the country's major estuaries where the land met the sea, but hundreds of other sites developed on the coasts and inland rivers. In 1881, there were no less than 643 separate sites at which cargoes might be loaded or discharged. Amongst these, London and Liverpool emerged as the two undisputed general cargo giants, their vast dock systems handling much of the British Empire's trade. Hull, the country's third port, and the other Humber ports of Grimsby, Immingham and Goole, also developed dock systems. Through them a wide variety of general goods, coal exports and timber imports passed. Both Hull and Grimsby also built docks for the vessels of their vast fishing fleets.

The long-established Atlantic port of Bristol overcame its locational problems by building the Avonmouth and Royal Edward Docks. At Glasgow, on the River Clyde, dock construction was triggered by the city's industrial boom, which provided exports including metal manufactures, cotton goods, chemicals, oils and paints and whisky. Inland from Liverpool, the Port of Manchester was established virtually overnight just prior

The huge growth of seaborne trade carried by an increasing number of merchant vessels was the driving force behind the great era of dock construction during the nineteenth and early twentieth centuries.

to the opening of the Manchester Ship Canal, which had been constructed by the Manchester Ship Canal Company between 1887 and 1894. This 36-mile long canal created a direct link between the industrial city and the sea, via the Mersey Estuary. In contrast, the docks at Southampton on the south coast grew on passenger trade. The port became home to several well-known shipping companies including P&O, the Royal Mail Steam Packet Company and White Star.

The expansion of Britain's coalfields drove dock building in many locations. The South Wales ports of Swansea, Cardiff, Barry, Penarth and Newport became major coal exporters, as did the Scottish ports of Burntisland, Methil and Grangemouth. Leith, the port of Edinburgh, also expanded on exported coal, but enjoyed a thriving general trade too. In close proximity to the coalfields of North East England, the Tyne was a major route for the export of coal, the largest coal staithes being located at Dunston in Gateshead, Hebburn, Tyne Dock and South Shields. Similar patterns of development occurred in response to the export of coal on Wearside at Sunderland and on the Tees at Middlesborough, although the latter also profited from the export of iron and steel from surrounding foundries.

In parallel with the expansion of large ports, smaller sites also developed. Railway companies in particular invested in new dock facilities at sites handling small ships in near-continental trades. Packet ports like Holyhead, Heysham, Ardrossan and Harwich were developed. In East Anglia the port of King's Lynn experienced the most notable growth, but other ports such as Boston, Wisbech, Ipswich and Lowestoft also acquired new facilities. Trade with Ireland triggered similar patterns of development in the North West at Silloth, Maryport, Fleetwood and Preston. In Scotland, Dundee and Kirkcaldy also experienced expansion, although construction at these two ports served local industry rather than the railways.

LABOURERS ON THE DOCKS: AGRICULTURAL LABOURERS, IRISH AND OTHERS

The great era of dock construction described in the previous section was a huge industrial undertaking and involved many people. Whilst engineers, architects and surveyors were the elites at the peak of this pyramid, thousands of navigational workers or 'navvies' provided the manpower and muscle to dig out dock basins, extensions and cuttings, shifting an almost unimaginable tonnage of earth. Such workers were mostly unskilled and had arrived in British ports seeking work in increasing numbers from the middle of the nineteenth century. Many stayed on to work the docks they had dug, having settled in dockside neighbourhoods nearby.

Irish navvies, like these pictured c. 1900, provided much of the muscle for the construction of Britain's emerging transport system including docks and railways.

A large number of these navvies-turned-dockers were originally agricultural labourers from the rural hinterlands surrounding port cities. Most, however, were migrants from Ireland. In the year following the first potato blight arrivals of Irish accelerated. The largest numbers settled in Liverpool, where some 300,000 men, women and children arrived on the docks in five months during 1847. However, it was the increasing economic opportunities available in the industrial towns of England, Scotland and Wales, coupled with the comparative poverty and inequality in Ireland, which encouraged the sustained arrival of Irish throughout the second half of the 1800s. The general pattern of migration saw emigrants from Ulster settle in Scotland, those from Connacht and the central strip of Ireland travelled via Dublin to Liverpool, while arrivals from Munster and other southerly or western areas sailed to South Wales, London or the English south coast.

In the towns and cities, where new large dock systems were being dug, general labourers from Ireland were used in abundance. This was certainly the case at the two general-cargo giants, London and Liverpool, but also at the Scottish ports of Glasgow, Dundee and Leith where Highlanders had also arrived in search of work. Even at the large east coast port of Hull there was a strong Irish presence on the docks. Consequently, large sections of the dock labour forces of many ports were dominated by the Irish, who were often separated from the general waterfront population both on and off the docks by their religion and clannish culture.

It [the kinship] went on from when they dug the docks out bloody centuries ago like but my grandparents were Irish they came from Ireland and they were part of the you-know that dug the docks out kind of thing – navvies and that's 'ow it all stemmed – the Catholics and they all stuck together . . . me brother-in-law when 'e married me sister 'e said that his father said 'those bloody Catholics' 'e said 'we can't ger a job on the dock' cos they used to go in the pubs – the local pubs that's where they got the jobs from when it first started centuries ago eighteen 'undred and odd. When all the immigrants were coming over from Ireland this is what I got told you see. They built the Catholic church and that's where my father went and me father went to that school and they built that for the Catholics and they knew that they were looking for work there and the Catholic church looked after them you see, in the old town? But you'd go on the dock and there was like Hegarty, Geraghty . . . I mean is family were Irish, 'e was a docker was Geraghty and then there was Phee – another one, all Irish families, all come from Irish people like, you know what I mean? Probably from centuries ago like eighteen 'undred and odd like my family. A lot of the foremen [were Irish] you could see like all Irish names – there was Hegarty and Flannery – that kind of thing – them old Irish names or O'Leary.

The emerging dock labour force of general labourers from rural areas and Ireland was supplemented by a third group. This was made up of a colourful variety of unemployed sailors, river workers and ex-soldiers along with an assortment of others who had fallen on hard times.

THE CASUAL SYSTEM

The employment arrangement of the dock labour force was highly unorthodox. The various port authorities who financed the building and operation of docks and port facilities provided quays, berths, cranes and warehouses for the movement of goods between ship and shore, they generally did not provide dock labour. Manchester and London were an exception, as both the Port of London Authority and the Manchester Ship Canal Company employed any dockers directly. Elsewhere, dock labour was largely employed by shipping companies either directly or via a wide variety of private waterfront employers, which included master stevedores, warehousemen and wharfingers. These firms commonly employed a number of permanent or 'regular' dock workers, but predominantly hired dockers on a casual basis to turn around (discharge and load) a single vessel. Once a ship had been turned-around the men would then seek another 'job'. This system, which survived until 1967, was a response to the varied, seasonal and generally fluctuating nature of seaborne trade. It allowed employers the flexibility to hire labour when trade was good yet not have the responsibility of paying them when trade dipped. Naturally, this placed the burden of underemployment on the dockers.

TYPES OF DOCK LABOURER

The country's wide variety of import and export trades and their associated cargo handling methods created a vast number of different occupations on the docks. A dock labourer or dock worker was the general term for anyone engaged on the various kinds of unskilled work in a dock such as carrying or wheeling goods from or to ships or assisting a highly-skilled category of docker known as a stevedore in the loading and unloading of vessels. However, there were dozens of sub-categories of dock labourer, which were often named in relation to the type of goods handled, their place of work or the specific skill(s) they performed in the cargo-handling process (see Glossary: Types of Dock Labourer). For example, carriers carried goods on their back, shoulder or head between quay, ship or warehouse or about the dock premises generally; they were usually specifically designated according to the goods they carried e.g. bag carrier, deal carrier, fish box carrier, fruit carrier. Alternatively, a filler was a dock labourer engaged in any filling operations in bulk into baskets or other receptacles in a ship's hold or on quay. In contrast, a hatchman or hatchwayman would stand by a ship's hatch when the vessel was loading or unloading and signal to a winchman when to set a winch in motion to raise or lower goods from or into the hold. A hatchman would signal with his hand to a holdsman when goods were about to be raised or lowered.

THE RECORDS

UK Census Records (see Chapter 1): UK census records are one of the best places to start when trying to find out where docker ancestors were born. Dock work frequently passed from father to son and it is often possible to trace generations of dockworkers back through the censuses (1841–1911). Although later generations may be recorded as having been born in the port where they resided and worked, the birth of an earlier ancestor

A gang of deal carriers at Hull c.1900. This type of dock worker specialized in the discharge and movement of timber 'deals'.

may indicate that the family originated from a rural area or Ireland. The 1841 census for England and Wales recorded whether a person was born in the county in which they were enumerated (Y or N) and whether they were born in Scotland (S) Ireland (I) or Foreign Parts (F). The 1851–1901 censuses recorded the county and parish of birth (if in England and Wales) as well as the country of Birth (if born outside England and Wales). The 1911 census provides even greater detail of nationality and exact birthplaces for people born in Scotland and Ireland. The census collection of Scotland follows a similar pattern to that of England and Wales in terms of the level of detail recorded about a person's place of birth.

Passenger Lists: Unfortunately, there are no passenger lists of people who crossed the Irish Sea by ship. Unlike those who left Ireland for Canada, the United States, Australia and New Zealand, Irish passengers bound for England, Scotland and Wales were not counted or recorded upon departure or arrival. This is because Ireland was part of Britain between 1801 and 1922 and the movement of peoples between the different parts of the British Isles was considered internal and therefore, unrestricted and unmonitored.

IRISH RECORDS

With such a large portion of the dock labour force originating from Ireland it is essential to establish where to find records relating to Irish ancestors. Many Irish genealogical records were destroyed in the early twentieth century, but most surviving material is divided between The National Archives of Ireland (NAI), National Library of Ireland (NLI) and the Public Record Office of Northern Ireland (PRONI):

The National Archives of Ireland (NAI)
Bishop Street, Dublin, D08 DF85
Tel: + 353 (0)1 407 2300
Email: query@nationalarchives.ie
Web: www.nationalarchives.ie

National Library of Ireland (NLI)
7–8 Kildare Street, Dublin 2, D02 P638
Tel: +353 1 603 02 00
Email: Info@nli.ie
Web: www.nli.ie

Public Record Office of Northern Ireland (PRONI)
2 Titanic Boulevard, Belfast, BT3 9HQ
Tel: 028 9053 4800
Email: proni@communities-ni.gov.uk
Web: www.nidirect.gov.uk/proni

Irish Censuses: The household returns and ancillary records for the censuses of Ireland of 1901 and 1911 are in the custody of the NAI and all thirty-two counties are available to search online at www.census.nationalarchives.ie/search. The 1901 and 1911 censuses are the only complete surviving census records for the pre-Independence period. Surviving census fragments and substitutes for 1821–51 are a valuable, if limited, resource for the pre-Famine period and can also be searched by year, surname, forename, county, barony (except 1821), parish and townland/street on NAI's website. Coverage includes:

> Antrim, 1851; Belfast city (one ward only), 1851; Cavan, 1821 and 1841; Cork, 1841; Dublin city (index to heads of household only), 1851; Fermanagh, 1821, 1841 and 1851; Galway, 1813 (numerical returns for Longford barony) and 1821; King's County (Offaly), 1821; Londonderry (Derry), 1831–4; Meath, 1821; Waterford, 1841.

Civil Registration of Birth, Marriages and Deaths in Ireland: A database of the civil registration indexes for the period 1845–1958 is free to search on www.familysearch.org/search/collection/1408347. All of Ireland is covered from 1845 until 1922 and the

Republic of Ireland from 1922 onwards. Copies of certificates for births, marriages and deaths occurring since 1 January 1864 (and Jewish and non-Roman Catholic marriages occurring since 1 April 1845) can be ordered from the General Registry Office in Dublin and local registry offices: www.welfare.ie/en/Pages/Apply-for-Certificates.aspx. For the six counties that comprise Northern Ireland (Antrim, Armagh, Down, Fermanagh, Londonderry/Derry and Tyrone) from 1922 onwards, records of births, marriages and deaths are held by the General Registry Office for Northern Ireland at Belfast. These can be ordered in a variety of ways, which are detailed at www.nidirect.gov.uk/articles/ordering-life-event-certificates. This General Register Office also holds all local register books for Northern Ireland from 1864 for births and deaths and from 1922 for marriages. In recent years millions of historic Irish births, deaths and marriage records have become available to the public online for the first time. More than 2.5 million images of old documents from the General Register Office can now be accessed for free at www.irishgenealogy.ie/en/. Images of the records currently cover:

- **Births, 1864–1915:** These include date and place of birth, name and sex of the child, name, surname and dwelling place of father, name, surname and maiden surname of mother, rank or profession of father, signature, qualification and residence of the informant, when registered and the signature of the registrar.

- **Marriages, 1882–1940:** Early marriage registers contain the date when married, name and surname of the spouses, their age, condition (i.e. marital status), rank or profession and residence at time of marriage, fathers' names, surnames and ranks or professions, where the marriage took place and by whom the marriage was witnessed and solemnised.

- **Deaths, 1891–1965:** Early death registers contain the date and place of death, name and surname of deceased, sex, condition, age last birthday, rank, profession or occupation of the deceased, certified cause of death and duration of illness, signature, qualification and residence of informant, when registered and the signature of the registrar.

Irish Parish Registers: Catholic parish registers recording baptism, marriage and death records throughout the whole of Ireland (including Northern Ireland) are held by the National Library of Ireland. These can be viewed free on Findmypast: www.findmypast.co.uk/irish-parish-records and with a subscription to Ancestry: https://search.ancestry.co.uk/search/db.aspx?dbid= 61039. Whilst baptism and marriage records make up the majority of the collection, death records can be found primarily for parishes in the northern regions. Registers containing records of baptisms and marriages for the majority of Catholic parishes in Ireland and Northern Ireland up to 1880 are also on The National Library of Ireland's own site: https:// registers.nli.ie. The start dates of the registers vary from the 1740 and 1750s in some city parishes in Dublin, Cork, Galway, Waterford and Limerick, to the 1780 and 1790s in counties such as Kildare, Wexford, Waterford and Kilkenny. Registers for parishes along the western seaboard do not generally begin until the 1850s and 1860s.

Irish Newspapers: The British Newspaper Archive offers a comprehensive online collection of local and national Irish titles www.britishnewspaperarchive.co.uk/titles/countries/ireland. This can also be accessed with a high tier subscription to Findmypast: https://search.findmypast.co.uk/search/irish-newspapers. A subscription to the Irish Newspaper Archive's website offers a comparable collection covering 1738 to present day: www.irish newsarchive.com/publication-list. Offline, the National Library of Ireland has the largest Irish newspaper archives in Ireland itself and also covers Northern Ireland. You can search its database www.nli.ie/en/catalogues-and-databases-printed-newspapers by either newspaper title or location, but to view the newspapers you have to visit the library. Dublin City Library and Archive also has an extensive holding of publications that include many of Ireland's one-time national titles as well as regional titles. PRONI holds a significant collection of nineteenth-century titles, specific titles can be searched on NLI's aforesaid catalogue.

RECOMMENDED READS

There is some very useful literature for those desirous of learning more about the development of particular ports. Arguably the best is *The History and Archaeology of Ports* (World's Work, 1983) by Gordon Jackson, although older books, David Owen's *The Origin and Development of the Ports of the United Kingdom* (Allman, 1948) and James Bird's *The Major Seaports of the United Kingdom* (Hutchinson, 1963) also cover the golden age of dock construction. *Dockers: The Impact of Industrial Change* (Fontana/ Collins, 1972) by David Wilson contains a very good chapter on the varied origins of the dockers and the companies that employed them. Wilson also covers the organization and nature of the casual system. Those with Irish ancestry on the docks can make use of Ian Maxwell's books *Your Irish Ancestors* (Pen and Sword, 2008) and *Tracing your Northern Irish Ancestors* (Pen and Sword, 2010). More specifically for researchers with Irish ancestors on the docks at Glasgow, William Kenefick's *Rebellious and Contrary: The Glasgow Dockers, 1853-1932* (Tuckwell Press Limited, 2000) is essential.

Chapter 3

DAILY LIFE ON THE DOCKS

At the heart of daily life on the docks was the casual system of employment. Whilst a number of 'regular' dockers were employed permanently by shipping companies or master stevedores and other dockside employers, the majority were 'casuals' who were hired to turn around (unload and reload) a ship. The casual system left employers with few obligations to their employees beyond payment, and as a result conditions and daily life on the docks were harsh. Such hardship, however, created tight-knit bonds amongst the labour force, which, coupled with a clannish nature, fostered a sense of brotherhood and indomitable spirit.

FIRST DAY ON THE JOB

Many dockers can recall their first day at work on the docks. Walking through the dock gates onto the dock estate, which was hidden behind the dock wall and something of a mystery to outsiders, would have been like entering a new world, somewhere different and separate from the rest of the town or city. Alongside dozens of sheds, warehouses and acres of cargoes stacked high, a new dock worker would have been surrounded by hundreds of workers, all similarly dressed in old suits, flat caps and mufflers tied in a 'docker's knot'. As dock work passed strictly from father to son, new dockers not only joined their parent but entire families. A father or other older dockers would show new recruits the ropes, with the expectation that they would be supported in their work during their old age on the docks.

[I started in] 1964, me twin started a few months before me. My elder brother was already on [the docks], my brother-in-law 'e was already on and my cousin 'e was already on. My uncle Bill was a docker, me uncle John was a docker, me cousin John was a docker and then I had other relations on there, stacks of relations but I didn't know 'alf of 'em cos there was that many men on there, you can't remember names. They had a flat hat on, docker's knot scarves and their coats on and they was *men*! And I loved 'em – the pubs where they went . . . and when I went on the dock it was like going in the old days! All the old sheds all the old ships . . . they still had ships gear, it was fantastic you-know! And I wanted that! And I loved that life! You just went on in a morning in what you 'ad on you and you stood there in the rain, sleet and blow, whatever you got there in, you wore all day. You always had to have a pair of them steel toe-cap boots cos it was a dangerous place and some days you'd get there and 'I ain't got a hook wi' me!' or if I got sent on a timber ship I dint have my tomahawk with me, or if I got sent carrying I dint have me apron or saddle with me, you needed them things with you really and you got some real good old fashioned dockers so they'd lend you one. The old dockers taught me everything!'

When I went on there, as soon as they found out 'oh are you Arthur's lad?!' Well they always thought that I was my eldest brother's lad cos they called him Arthur and my dad Arthur and I said 'no, I'm Arthur's brother' and they said 'come on you're alright we'll show you' and they showed me everything what to do, how to make things easy for me, that's what they did. They were very, very good.

Dockers at work on the deck of a ship at Whitehaven Harbour.

EMPLOYERS AND THE ALLOCATION OF WORK

The casual system ensured that many dock workers were not tied to a single employer. Indeed, most dock workers would work for dozens of different employers during their working life. By 1960 there were some 1,500 employers of dock labour across the ports for a labour force of around 70,000 men. Such companies varied greatly in terms of their size. Scruttons Ltd of London, for example, employed around 3,000 men, while other firms did as little as one job a year, employing just a handful of men. The day-to-day business of hiring, directing and overseeing of the dockers' work was the responsibility of the employers' foremen. A foreman would hire the required number of casual dockers at the call to supplement his permanent workers [should any be employed]. The number hired was dependent upon the volume and nature of cargo in question. The hiring process for casual workers commonly took place at the dock gates, or at other designated areas on or around the docks such as the gangway of a vessel. The employer's foreman would then select the appropriate number of dockers. Later, following the introduction of the National Dock Labour Scheme Scheme, hiring took place at designated hiring halls known as controls (see Chapter 8).

There were mixed feelings amongst dockers about the casual hiring process, particularly at ports that paid workers by the piece. At these ports, dockers' rates of pay were determined by the type and volume of cargo as well as the method of handling. Naturally, the best-paying jobs were most desired. Some dockers felt that, more often than not, well-paid work was distributed to so-called 'blue-eyed boys' due to either bribery or favouritism. Others believed it was the best workers who were awarded the better jobs by foremen, due to their ability to turn around ships quickly. At most ports there was also bitter divisions between casual and regular men, the former often envious of the latter's more secure and respectable status.

> Sometimes they got the job the night before in the boozer and the foreman was in there, get all his beer free and 'yeah, you'll be on in morning and you'll be alright' and what'd 'appen the following morning they all went to go to what they called the gangway end and . . . well the side of the ship anyhow – the gangway and he could pick his men who he wanted. Them was the blue-eyes – the relations and 'I saw your wife last night – you can have a job' and that you-know [Laughs]. Well these are the stories that went on. It was all booze and God-knows. Well I lived down a street where they 'ad these local boozers and the foreman used to sit there and he'd just sit in the snug there on his own and there was all his beer lined up there! He used to sit there and sup, he never used to buy one. People hoped they'd get a job in the morning – it was rife!'

The blue-eyes – they were prepared to work! The other buggers didn't wanna know, to be honest! The foremen went in and he picked his men and he didn't pick people that didn't bloody work! He had to get the ship finished. Stevedoring is quite simple – you pay everything out by the hour or by time and you get paid by the ton – so you only make a profit if you turn it around quick enough. If you don't turn the bugger round you don't make a profit!

George Orwell's diary recorded 'the call' at Liverpool docks in 1936:

When we got there we found about 200 men waiting in a ring and Police holding them back. It appeared that there was a fruit ship needed unloading and on the news that there had been jobs going there had been a fight between the dockers which the police had to intervene to stop. After a while the agent of the company (known as the stevedore, I think) emerged from a shed and began calling out the names or rather numbers of the gangs whom he had engaged earlier in the day. Then he needed about 10 men more, and walked round the ring picking out a man here and there. He would pause, select a man, take a man by the shoulder and haul him forward, exactly as at a sale of cattle. Presently he announced that was all. A sort of moan went up from the remaining dockers, and they trailed off, about 50 men having been engaged out of 200. It appears that unemployed dockers have to sign on twice a day, otherwise they are presumed to have been working (as their work is mainly casual labour, by the day) and their dole docked for that day.

CARGO-HANDLING

Between the 1840s and the early 1960s there had been only partial progress in the way seaborne goods were handled at

British ports. Nineteenth-century advancements in cargo-handling included the introduction of cranes, hoists, conveyors, grabs, elevators and mechanical slings. However, this equipment related to specific bulk trades. Mechanized means were not always used for bulk goods when expensive dock dues for mechanized berths made it cheaper to employ manual labour. Furthermore, there was virtually no mechanical development in the handling of general goods. During the early 1960s most miscellaneous goods and commodities still came or went in 'man-sized' boxes, barrels and packages, which were carried by gangs of dockers between a ship and warehouses or waiting landward transport, initially barges and carts and later railway wagons and motor vehicles. Consequently, most dock work was labour-intensive, dirty and physically arduous. Again, a factor here was the casual system, which discouraged employers from investing money in machinery when cheap manual labour could be hired and then discarded. The container revolution that swept away manual cargo handling virtually overnight in the mid-1960s will be discussed in Chapter 9.

> With the lighters what they used to do as well was bagged cargos, they used to weigh it on the deck and they used to rip it and send it down a shoot so they know how much tonnage was in the lighter – 'ripping and tipping', they had a tallyman on the scale and they used to come over in sets of five or seven or whatever, they used to drop it on the scale and they used to have the big weights and they used to weigh it off and then mark it up in the book and then over. And when you got x number of tons – say they wanted 250 tons you'd be totting up as you went along – page by page – carry it forward – then you'd say '250 ton that's it!', cover up bring in the next one but of course you had the number of the craft and the name of the craft so you could tell 'em how much was in that craft and then next one would come in and you'd call the next one in and that's how it went.

Whitehaven dockers in the hold of a vessel discharging a loose bulk cargo with shovels.

With the Copenhagen ship I worked with a team mostly – called the 'hungry eight' – all six feet tall. In them days with the bacon we used to stack it five high. I could lift it –

A general cargo vessel berthed.

between sixteen and eighteen stone, I could lift 'em up like that myself! And your butter, what you did with your butter – your eight stone barrels of butter – you rolled 'em out and then you put another tier on the top and just chucked the you-know and that was for eight, ten hours a day!'

It all had to be carried off, the timber 'ad to be slung onto the ship then landed onto these stages and carried off. I've worked down there a few times. I want a deal carrier but you 'ad to go down and do the job and you used to look down and I used to think to myself . . . cos it was a really busy dock when all the timber used to come in and I used to look down and think they'd 'ave been doin' this job 200 years ago. In fact, they wun't let you alter cos you was on piece work and I know one particular ship we could have landed lofty derricks . . . what they call lofty derricks – long derricks and we could have landed... made the sets on the ship and landed it in the wagons or on the bogies and we did it a couple of times and 'whoa stop the job, stop the job – you can't do that, they've got to be lifted and carried' cos we'd have gone through the roof with our wages being on piece work. So they wouldn't let us do that.

ACCIDENTS, INJURIES AND DISEASES

Manual methods of handling cargoes, which were occasionally toxic, made dock work an incredibly dangerous occupation. Employers had little, if any, obligation to provide their casuals with safety equipment or clothing and dockers were often simply clad in flat caps, long jackets and boots. Heavy goods were lifted in and out of ships' holds high above the heads of workers. Cargoes frequently fell and crushed those below, whilst wires and ropes attached to cranes often snapped, swinging cargoes dangerously towards hapless dockers. Workers would also suffer paralysis and death due to falling from decks deep into the holds of ships. Alongside these hazards was the risk of contracting illnesses from the handling of toxic cargoes such as sulphur and asbestos or anthrax from animal hides.

There was a big accident rate, the first week I was on the dock there was a bloke killed. A becket 'ad gone – 'ad broken and 'ad swung right at this bloke. It'd been shackled, so a thin, a wire becket and you'd put it through the shackle and the shackle would be attached to the line that would pull the grab in and the wire becket had broken and the shackle 'ad flew across the hold and 'it this bloke in the chest and caved his ribs in. 'e died and that was my first week on the dock that you-know. There was always accidents on the dock.

I've seen 'em killed with winches falling and hitting 'em, I've seen kids fall down the hold, I've fell down twice . . . me back . . . in the end I had to have an operation on my back but yes there's been some accidents and a lot of kids fell down the hold. One docker he fell down the hold and he dint fall very far and he was completely wheelchair

DOCKER CRUSHED TO DEATH.

George Catton (22), married, 2, Spring Street, Middlesbrough, was crushed to death on the Tyne-Tees shipping company's wharf, Middlesbrough, last night.

With three other men he was engaged in loading boxes of salt to the s.s. Middlesbrough with the aid of an electric crane. For some reason, Catton went to the hatch and leaned over the bogey turn of the crane. The crane swerved into the ship, crushing Catton severely. He fell off the ship on to the quay, and was taken to the North Ormesby Infirmary but was dead on arrival.

A newspaper report on the death of a Middlesbrough docker. Leeds Mercury *and* Yorkshire Post, *22 February 1934.*

bound. I don't know how he did it but it was only on a very small ship and all, he didn't fall far but people can go a long way down. Another docker 'e used to love night fishing, 'e used to come straight to work from night fishing and 'e was on the same ship as me – *Debrovsky* and we was down in the hold – two holds deep it was and they was working above and we'd emptied the hold and we was waiting for stuff to start loading and one of the crew members leant against what you call a railing you-know like a guard and the ship was that rusty and it just collapsed and went down and they shouted 'RUN!!' and everybody down below run one way barring this docker – 'e ran the other way and it hit him straight on his head and that kid was never the same kid – it hit him right on the head. There was also a lot of leg injuries – men trapped with timber and steel. It was hazardous to think back how many accidents.

NICKNAMES

Working in gangs in conditions that were often dangerous or insanitary, dockers everywhere shared a strong sense of camaraderie. Amongst the thousands of workers on the docks, there were many characters whose humour or eccentricities would keep up morale. In all ports, dockers christened one another and foremen with nicknames based on particular traits, often favourite catchphrases or mannerisms. In fact, it is widely said that some men worked alongside each other for years never actually knowing their friends' real names. The following are some of the nicknames used by dockers at Liverpool, some are more cryptic than others:

Van Gough: 'Let me put you in the picture lads'
The Sherriff: 'Where's the hold-up?'
The Drug Addict: 'I got some morphia (more for yer), lads'
High Noon: 'Shooting off at twelve'
Lino: 'He's always on the floor'
The Balloon: 'Don't let me down lads'
Dr Jekyll: 'I need a change'
Batman: 'Never leaves a ship without robbin''
The Gunner: 'I was gunner do that'
Parish Priest: 'He only works Sundays'
Phil the Cot: 'Father of many'
Wonder Boy: 'I wonder what that is'
The Surgeon: 'Cut it out lads'
The Zookeeper: 'I'm a bit cagey about this'
Olympic Torch: 'Never goes out'
Sick Lobster: 'I'm off home my nippers are ill'
Pontius Pilate: 'Always washing his hands'
The Undertaker: 'Lay 'em out over there'
Harpic: 'Clean round the bend'
Al Capone: 'Where's me gang'

PROTECTIVE PRACTICES: THE 'WELT' AND 'SPELLING'

The introduction of port working agreements gave dockers an increased degree of control on the docks and in most ports, where men had suffered poor pay and the evils of the casual system for decades, dockers would also take part in various practices designed to protect against the insecurity of casualism. To employers, however, such habits were considered restrictive or wasteful. Many deplored them as they seriously hampered productivity and increased costs that were passed on to the shipping company whose vessel they were contracted to turn around.

Regardless of whether viewed as protective or restrictive the practices were part of a port's custom and a part of daily life on the docks. One example, was the dockers' insistence on higher-than-necessary manning scales. This ensured increased employment with more men being hired at the call. As more men were hired than were necessary, practices like 'the welt' or 'spelling' were common-place. The welt emerged during the First World War and involved half a gang absenting itself from work for a period and the other half leaving when the first returned. Few dockers denied taking part in the welt and would admit to disappearing for a couple of hours, but employers regularly complained that men they had hired would spend all day in nearby pubs or working second jobs like window cleaning rounds or driving taxis. Another tactic amongst dockers was the 'go-slow'. Once hired, dockers largely had control of their own work in the hold, on the quay and in the warehouse and they could control the rate of loading and discharge, even bringing work to a stop. This was intended to increase earnings amongst the gang. Dockers would often halt a job and insist on being paid pre-agreed bonus payments for things like working dirty, wet or difficult cargoes. They would also demand restrictions on the grounds of safety such as reducing the volume goods in a sling load. Aside from this dockers would often take extended tea breaks in the hope that their work would spin into overtime.

A group of Grimsby and Immingham dockers at work discharging bagged goods.

We used to start at 8 o'clock in a morning when I first got me dockers' book. We started at 8 in a morning, then at quarter to nine you'd go to mugger – what they called coffee shop till about half past nine, worked till half 11 then you'd all stop for dinner. There was what they called a lot of 'restrictive practices'. See you get a ship and they'd say 'right, we want 6 men for that part of the ship and six men for that part of the ship' and we'd start the cargo. But the construction of the ships and the type of cargo you couldn't get six men in that working space to start with till you got what they called a 'break-down'. And we used to say 'well, us two'll start the ship and you to have a couple of hours whatever you like' . . . on pay . . . and then they'd come back. Obviously the owners didn't like that. They'd rather have had the four men – paid four men they called it 'restrictive practices' so there was a lot of that went on.

LEISURE AND AMENITIES

Whilst working conditions were harsh, dock workers had access to few, if any, amenities on the docks. Neither employers of dock labour or port authorities provided dockers with simple but necessary facilities such as canteens, toilets and lockers, basic amenities that were common in many other large industries. In the absence of canteens, dockside cafes and coffee shops provided dockers with food, drink and shelter during breaks, periods of unemployment and bad weather. Often ramshackle and unsanitary, such places were notorious and many stories about them abound amongst former dock workers. Places like Frank's Café in Liverpool and the Klondyke Café in Hull had a busy and bustling atmosphere as dockers congregated and shared stories, jokes and interests. More importantly, such places served hearty, high-calorie foods, which the dockers required to fuel their physically gruelling work.

Dockers' cafes were an essential part of life on the docks.

There was these two little brick places with the toilets in and they was always . . .and I don't know if they ever got cleaned . . . I mean it was frozen solid [in the winter] . . . I mean the toilets was atrocious and the coffee shops was like the Black 'ole of Calcutta it was terrible – filthy, mucky places you-know. They had a little fire in the middle and the old dockers used to stand gettin' warm round it.

Some of 'em honestly were unbelievable in the earlier times. I mean there was birds flyin' about all over, there was water dripping through the roof [Laughs] it was a bit rough at the time . . . for everyone but everyone got by, everybody 'ad a laugh.'

There was laughter on the dock – it was hard, it was dirty, it was bad and you went in the coffee shops there and in the winter time they 'ad a big fire in there and that was dirty. Your boots was dirty and, you see, when you left, the rats went back in again, you see? but the conditions then you just took 'em for granted.

I was with my mate and we went in [to the coffee shop] Anyway we was queuing up and Hilly – Hills – who owned the place and my mate said 'Look! There's a bloody rat there!' and I looked and there was a rat on back of the . . . on one of the tops and 'e said 'look at that!' and he said 'Oh that's Pinky and Perky' [Laughs]. So I said 'Oh well, I aren't buying owt in here, I'll just 'ave a cup o' tea'.

Like anywhere else a lot kept racing pigeons and we'd all gather together in the coffee shops and all 'avin' a chat about the best bird [Laughs] and then there was the gardeners you see and I started being interested in gardening through talking to people on the docks. I 'adn't a clue about gardening at the time. Talking to people and got interested and that's one of the things I do now and I've won competitions with me gardening in the past.

THE RECORDS
On Film: British Transport Films' docu-drama *Berth 24* (1950) provides arguably the best visual portrayal of daily life on the docks. The 40-minute film is a semi-dramatized account of the turn around of Ellerman's Wilson Line vessel S.S. *Bravo* at Hull's Alexandra Dock. Every aspect of the dockers' day is covered. This includes their scramble for work at the morning call, the foreman's organization of his gangs and their work discharging a wide variety of cargoes to the quays, warehouses and waiting landward transport. The second half of the film shows the same

process in reverse with the foreman planning the vessel's loading and the stowage of goods by the dockers. Many of the cargoes and various cargo-handling methods are depicted in the film including the work of deal carriers and coal trimmers. The film is available to view on the British Film Institute's website www.screenonline.org.uk/film/id/705128/ or on the widely available DVD *'Just the Ticket': British Transport Films collection, Volume 9*.

Local Trade Directories: Local trade directories from the nineteenth and twentieth centuries are excellent starting points for identifying the employers of both permanent and casual dock labourers. Volumes commonly list the names and addresses of master stevedores, shipping companies, warehousemen and wharfingers, alongside the various other companies that employed dock labour. Series such as Kelly's Directory are widely available at local and county archives. City and county directories, for the nineteenth and twentieth centuries can be accessed online with a subscription to Ancestry at https://search.ancestry.co.uk/search/db.aspx?dbid=1547.

Newspapers (see Chapter 1): Accessed either at local archives or online, newspapers are the best record set for those trying to find out more about accident and injuries suffered by their dock worker ancestors. Newspapers often reported on serious accidents on the docks and, in cases of fatality, information regarding inquests and their verdicts can also be found.

RECOMMENDED READS
There are a small number of very useful books available, which cover various aspects of daily life on the docks of the larger ports. Henry T. Bradford, *Tales of London's Docklands* (The History Press, 2007) is a compilation of stories based on the author's personal experiences on London's docks and the East End, whilst Albert

G. Linney, *Peepshow of the Port of London* (Sampson Low, Marston and Co., 1930) provides a detailed insight of an outsider into the world of the capital's dockers. *The Dock Worker: An Analysis of Conditions of Employment in the Port of Manchester* (Liverpool University Press, 1954) is a sociological study and one of the most detailed insights into a dock labour force during the 1950s. For cargo-handling practices at specific ports see Mary Greenough, *Cargo Handling in the Port of Liverpool in the 1920s* (National Museums and Galleries on Merseyside, 1981) and for London see Robert B. Oram, *Cargo Handling and the Modern Port* (Pergamon Press, 1965). For those wishing to delve deeper into the cargo handling activities of their docker ancestor Peter Brodie, *Illustrated Dictionary of Cargo Handling* (Routledge, 2015) is essential.

Chapter 4

TOOLS AND EQUIPMENT

Unlike most other historic industries, particularly those in trades and manufacturing industries, there are only a few objects associated with dock work. As established in the previous chapter, the casual system left employers with little obligation to provide anything beyond pay to their workers. Consequently, no uniforms, overalls, hard hats, gloves or boots were issued. In reality, it was muscle and movement that was central to the job and dockers arrived at the call with little more than the clothes they stood in. Dockers did, however, use a number of tools that were specifically designed or adapted for moving goods on the docks. Such tools were often unique and could not be found in any other industries. Following the widespread introduction of mechanized means of cargo handling from the 1960s (see Chapter 9) the traditional tools of dockland were rendered redundant.

The first part of this chapter introduces many of the common dockland tools and describes their function. Many dockers kept their old tools, particularly their hand hooks, some of which had been passed down through generations. Some family historians may be lucky enough to inherit objects associated with dock work that have been kept by docker ancestors. Such items are not only personal treasures that provide physical links to one's familial past, they can also be excellent sources of information about the everyday work of those who once toiled on the waterfront. Researchers not fortunate enough to inherit memorabilia can still access and learn much from historical dockland objects displayed by museums, both in physical exhibits and online collections as detailed in the second part of this chapter.

HAND HOOKS

The dockers' principle tool for working man-sized general cargoes was the steel hand hook, which symbolized the docking occupation more than any other object. Indeed, it is possible that the phrase to 'Sling your hook' originated on the docks when foremen dismissed those casual dockers not hired for work at the call. Hooks were used to grip, lift and pull goods or direct slings loaded with goods between ship and inland transport or warehouses. Hooks varied in terms of their size, curvature and handle, depending on the cargo being handled i.e. bags, bails, crates etc.

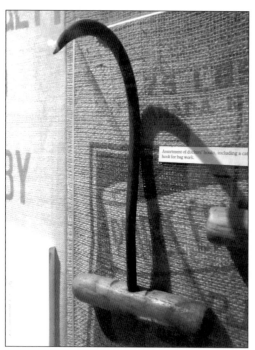

Another type of dockers' 'S' hook, belonging to Hull docker Trevor Green.

A classic type of dockers' 'S' hook with a wooden handle.

This type of dockers' hook was known as a 'case hook'.

Cat's paw hook, also known as a 'scratcher', had a metal pad for gripping bags and sacks.

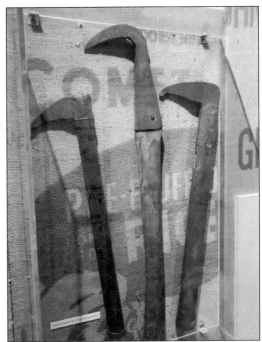

Tomahawk or timber hook, this tool was used to drag timber.

Docker's double bag hook with wooden handle. Used to lift fine or delicate bagged cargoes.

[Pit props were covered in] thick grease and you teck a wire and you'd try to get what they call a 'nose-ender' which is, you work the wire along the pit-props and you've got an 'S' hook – one end in the wire and the other wire going round the other end, and it was supposed to nip tight as the crane takes the weight of it. Well they're was greasy as hell and slide all over the bleedin' place, as it's goin' up you've got to be dodgin' as well like . . .

49

FORKS AND SHOVELS

Shovels and forks were used by dockers to break down and shift loose bulk cargoes that had become impacted in the ships hold.

> Copra is the dry husks of coconut and it was just one heap of crawling cockroaches and things like that and there were all sorts of flies. Richard [*sic*]Attenborough could have done a good programme in a copra ship [Laughs] and it used to be stinking hot inside and the method of discharge was – we'd go into the hold with shovels and picks, loosen all the copra up and a grab would come and grab the coconut out and at the end when we'd took the majority of the cargo out we had to shovel out all the corners, wings and lockers you had to shovel all this out – well by then it'd gone to a slimy oily mess it was and that wasn't a very nice job at all.

A docker's fork.

A docker's shovel.

DISHES, PANS AND SCUTTLES

Dishes or scuttles were most commonly used at grain-handling ports. Dockers would often stand waist-deep in grain in the holds of ships and scoop the grain into bags. The first pneumatic grain elevators were introduced at London's Millwall Docks around 1892, in an early example of mechanized cargo handling. As elevators became more common at other grain-handling ports during the first half of the twentieth century, hand-scuttling became less common. Nevertheless, the practice was still in use at some ports, like Hull, during the 1950s.

When I first come on the dock you 'ad to do filling and they'd give you a five bushel bag which stood about this height and they'd give you a big fryin' . . . we used to call 'em fryin' pans . . . like a big dish – [about as big as a] dart board maybe a little bit bigger than that and it was a dish like that . . . and one bloke – 'e used to 'old the bag down there and 'e used to go 'one, two . . . ' and as you put more in and 'e used to come up with it like that there and you could get – if you did it right – about nine and half scoops in a bag and that was your 12 bushels.

A grain pan or scuttle.

SHOULDER SADDLES

At timber-handling ports, like London and Hull, wooden planks or 'deals' were carried ashore on the shoulders of highly-skilled dockers known as deal carriers or deal porters. To protect them from splinters and abrasions, these workers wore thick leather shoulder saddles. The saddle only offered some protection to the carriers, many of whom would develop a rough callus or hard lump on the shoulder from the chafing of their shirt, saddle and the timber. It was often said that long-serving deal carriers could be identified in the street by their lopsided shoulders, their carrying shoulder hanging noticeably lower than the other after years of heavy carrying.

Deal carriers using leather shoulder saddles c. 1950.

Leather shoulder saddle commonly used by deal carriers.

SACK BARROWS AND HAND TRUCKS
Bagged goods such as sugar, grain, copra, flour and tobacco were commonly moved between quays, warehouses and land transport via wooden sack barrows, otherwise known as hand trucks.

MUSEUM COLLECTIONS
For those researchers not fortunate enough to inherit or own dockland memorabilia, some

A two-handled wood and iron sack barrow.

items are available to view in the exhibits and online collections of a small number of museums:

Museum of London Docklands

No. 1 Warehouse, West India Quay, London, E14 4AL
Tel: 020 7001 9844
Web: www.museumoflondon.org.uk/museum-london-docklands
The Museum of London Docklands is situated on the Isle of Dogs, east London and tells the history of the River Thames and the growth of its docklands. The museum hosts some excellent galleries and exhibits relating to dockers and dock work including 'No. 1 Warehouse', 'Warehouse of the World (1880–1939)', 'Docklands at War (1939–1945)' and 'New Port, New City'. The Museum also has a large online collection of dock related objects that are not on physical display: www.museumoflondon.org.uk/collections. Search terms such as 'docker', 'dock worker', 'docks' and 'stevedore' are very fruitful.

National Maritime Museum

Park Row, Greenwich, London, SE10 9NF
Tel: 020 8858 4422
Web: www.rmg.co.uk/national-maritime-museum
The museum's exhibits represent the elite and military, rather than the labouring, aspects of Britain's maritime heritage. However, its online catalogue: http://collections.rmg.co.uk/ does contain objects, photographs and paintings relating to docks and dock work. The museum also houses the Caird Library and Archive, which holds original documents and publications about dock workers: www.rmg.co.uk/national-maritime-museum/caird-library. Nearby is the nineteenth-century clipper *Cutty Sark*, a museum ship that offers an excellent and rare opportunity to explore a trading vessel of the type worked by dockers, particularly in London: www.rmg.co.uk/cutty-sark.

Historic dock cranes at London's Docklands.

Hull Maritime Museum

Little Queen Street, Hull, HU1 3DX

Tel: 01482 300300

Email: museums@hcandl.co.uk

Web: www.hcandl.co.uk/museums-and-galleries/hull-maritime-museum

Hull's Maritime Museum is housed in the city's former dock offices, built in 1872. Alongside the museum's exhibits on the port's fishing and whaling heritage, the Docking Gallery contains an excellent display of tools, equipment and information relating to dock work and the dockers' union. The museum's online collection: http://museums.hullcc.gov.uk/ also features some objects from The Marfleet Collection, possibly the largest assemblage of dock workers tools in the country. The collection

The Docking Gallery at Hull's Maritime Museum.

was created by local barber Walter Oglesby and is made up from dozens of items donated by dockers who patronised his dockside barbershop.

M Shed (Bristol)

Princes Wharf, Wapping Road, Bristol, BS1 4RN
Tel: 0117 352 6600
Web: www.bristolmuseums.org.uk/m-shed/
Bristol's M Shed Museum displays some rare working examples of the docks cranes that were used prior to the introduction of modern cargo-handling methods. There are two electric cranes, which are the last survivors of eight that were originally on Bristol's quayside, and of over forty which were originally in the port's City Docks during the 1950s. The museum also displays the Fairbairn steam crane. Built in 1878, it is the oldest surviving exhibit of its type in Britain and is a scheduled ancient monument. The cranes are working exhibits and at certain times it is possible to see them in operation on the museum's 'crane rides'.

National Waterfront Museum

Oystermouth Road, Maritime Quarter, Swansea, SA1 3RD
Tel: 0300 111 2333
Email: waterfront@museumwales.ac.uk
Web: https://museum.wales/swansea/
The museum charts the industrial and transport history of Wales and features exhibits relating to dock work, particularly in the Sea Gallery, where historic film and items relating to the coal trimmers that dominated the South Wales ports can be found. Coal trimmers and other maritime objects also feature in the Coal Gallery, whilst some exhibits relating to dock unionism are covered in the 'Organization' section. The museum also has a good online collection with a varied selection of paintings, photographs, anniversary medals, and registration and union cards: https://museum.wales/collections/online/.

Chapter 5

TRADE UNIONS

The insecurity and exploitation associated with casual employment on the docks fostered a strong sense of unity and militancy amongst the dock workers. Indeed, there are few, if any, groups more strongly associated with trade unionism and industrial action than the dockers. The story of trade unionism on the docks is long and complicated and much has been written about the subject. In order to make sense of labour organization on the waterfront, the first half of this chapter establishes the roots, development and activities of the various dockers' unions that were central to the working life of each and every dock worker. Trade union records by bar far the greatest collection of documentary sources relating to the dockers, and the second half of this chapter provides a guide on where they can be found.

ORIGINS OF WATERFRONT UNIONISM
Evidence of the first stirrings of unionism on Britain's docks can be traced to the middle of the nineteenth century. In Scotland, the Glasgow dockers had established the Glasgow Harbour Labourers' Union as early as 1853, whilst the year 1858 inscribed on a banner entitled 'Dockers of Leith' indicates the presence of union in that port around the same time. The Leith dockers had formed a new union by 1866 named the Leith Dock and Harbour Labourers' Union. Within a few weeks of its creation the Leith union went on strike over a claim for increased wages. In London, the stevedores and dockers organized themselves under the

Labour Protection League in 1872. At the time, trade was booming in the Port of London and, with employment high and dock labour in demand, the league made huge progress by winning a series of wage increases and gaining a membership of around 20,000. The formation of these early unions was undoubtedly an important step in the organization of the dockers, however, it failed to gain a strong foothold for unionism on the docks.

A trade union banner of the Leith Dockers dated 1858. Image courtesy of The City of Edinburgh Council; Museums and Galleries.

THE GREAT DOCK STRIKE, 1889

The Great Dock Strike of August 1889, often referred to as the London Dock Strike, not only marked the beginnings of strong unionism in the port industry but also heralded the new unionism of unskilled and semi-skilled workers. Amidst the growing discontent of London's casual dockers regarding the danger, low pay and poor conditions, the strike was sparked by a relatively minor dispute over a bonus payment to a group of dock workers who were unloading a vessel named *Lady Armstrong* at the South-West India Dock. A key organizer behind the subsequent action that unfolded was Ben Tillett, a dock worker who two years earlier had established the Tea Operatives and General Labourers'

Association for dockers involved in handling cargoes of tea. On the heels of the incident at the South-West India Dock, hundreds of dockers joined the Association established by Tillett, who subsequently requested pay of 6 pence per hour (the 'Docker's Tanner'), with 8 pence per hour overtime and a minimum payment equivalent to 4 hours wages for the casual dockers taken on each morning. With no response received from the dock companies by 14 August, the strike became official. A few days later the union was renamed the Dock, Wharf, Riverside and General Workers' Union (DWRLU).

Despite its dramatic birth and rise, the union experienced a serious downturn after 1891. Initially, 30,000 members had enrolled into the new union and this had risen to 57,000 in 1890, when 63 new branches had been formed around the country. However, a downturn in trade, coupled with a fierce employer offensive, caused a membership decline. By the end of 1894, membership across the country was just 10,600. By 1904 the DWRLU, which had been renamed the Dock, Wharf, Riverside and General Workers' Union of Great Britain and Ireland in 1899, had almost disappeared from London, although its presence did remain strong elsewhere.

Outside the capital there were trade union developments at the other ports. In the same year as the strike, the National Union of Dock Labourers (NUDL) was founded in Glasgow. The NUDL's first annual conference was held in the city during the following year, however, the 1891 conference was moved to Liverpool, where a large number of the union's membership resided. The English members proposed moving the union's headquarters to Liverpool and their superior numbers carried the day, much to the consternation of the Glaswegian dockers who feared that their interests would be neglected. The Glasgow branch of the NUDL continued, but closed in December 1910. The Following year the Glasgow dockers established the Scottish Union of Dock Labourers (SUDL). By this time, a great deal of progress had been made regarding the organization of dock workers. However, the unions were largely regional and the dockers lacked the national organization, particularly between the large dock labour forces at London and Liverpool, which would strengthen their position within the port industry. Over 20 years on from the Great Dock Strike in London, the wages of the country's dockers had barely risen.

THE 1911 STRIKES

The first great step in achieving national union organization on the docks came in 1910. In that year Ben Tillett, the union organizer who had risen to prominence in the Great Dock Strike of 1889, formed the National Transport and Workers Federation (NTWF). Within a year a wave of transport strikes, largely coordinated by the NTWF, swept the country and involved 100,000 workers. In Liverpool, the dockers went on strike with the port's sailors and railway workers and brought the docks to a virtual standstill. Agreements between employers and unions across the country were reached, although industrial peace was temporary. More strikes followed in London in 1912, but support around the rest of the country was limited. The onset of the First World War, which drew thousands of dockers away from the ports, put paid to the industrial unrest of the previous years (see Chapter 7).

THE FIRST REFORMS: REGISTRATION SCHEMES

Following the Great Dock Strike in 1889 the registration of dock workers was introduced to ensure that dock work was reserved for dedicated dockers rather than the general floating mass of casual labour that wandered the waterfront in search of work. Furthermore, registration ensured that employers had access to a steady and organized pool of labour. The first registration schemes were developed and introduced at London and Liverpool. The London plan was suggested by the social reformer

Charles Booth and implemented by the London and India Docks Company in 1891. Known as 'Mr Booth's Scheme', it divided the port's labour force into four categories:

- **Permanent Staff:** This group were paid weekly, given a paid holiday, sick benefit and a benevolent allowance of up to 10 shillings after 15 years' service.

- **A List:** These dockers formed a group from which the permanent men were recruited. They were guaranteed a week's work at a time when accepted for work at the call and were given priority of employment the B List men. The A List was abolished in the First World War.

- **B List:** The B List men were ordinary causal dockers but had a preference ticket and filled gaps in the A List.

- **C List:** The men of the C List were out-and-out casuals who often followed a particular foreman who they hoped would hire them for work based on their loyal service.

The Liverpool scheme differed greatly from the London version, but its intended effect of better organizing the port's labour force was the same. Known as the 'Tally System', the Liverpool scheme was introduced in July 1912 and registered all of the port's dockers, each of whom was given a metal 'tally', and it was agreed that only those with a tally could be given work. An added feature of the scheme was its joint control by a committee made up of equal numbers of officials from the National Union of Dock Labourers and employers' representatives. The committee's principal task was to control the issuing of new tallies and the organization of fourteen surplus stands where men not hired at the morning call were to report.

The huge upheaval of the First World War highlighted the need for the better organization of dock labour across the country's ports. By the early 1930s thirty-one major ports had registration schemes of which twenty-five were jointly controlled by union and employer representatives. By the start of the Second World War only the ports of Glasgow and Aberdeen were without schemes. Not all categories of docker were registered; coal trimmers were generally excluded and in some ports, so too were deal porters. An important feature of many of the schemes across the ports was that dockers' sons were given preference when new dockers were registered. This made dock work largely a closed shop across much of the industry.

THE TRANSPORT AND GENERAL WORKERS' UNION

The largest and most powerful union in the history of the docks, and indeed the country, was the Transport and General Workers' Union (TGWU). The TGWU was established on 1 January 1922 following the amalgamation of fourteen unions from the transport industry, which involved several docks unions including the Dock, Wharf, Riverside and General Labourers' Union of Great Britain and Ireland. One of the founding leaders of the TGWU and its first general secretary was Ernest Bevin, who went on to be appointed wartime Minister of Labour and later Foreign Secretary in the post-war Labour government. In the TGWU's first year other dockers' unions from around Britain voted to amalgamate including the Scottish Union of Dock Labourers and the National Union of Dock Labourers, which, by then, had been renamed the National Union of Dock, Riverside and General Workers in Great Britain and Ireland.

Following its creation and growth, the TGWU was far from unified. Most rank-and-file dockers were increasingly distrustful of the union's officials who were chosen by union leaders rather than being elected by the rank and file. Many on the docks believed that, more often than not, officials sided with the employers of dock labour. During the 1930s a number of incidents at Hull involving a 'wreckers gang' who had links with the TGWU provides one example of how the rift between officials and the rank and file was exacerbated. The wreckers were organized by existing employers to prevent new stevedoring firms setting up on the docks. Hard men from amongst the dockers were organized to 'wreck' the newcomers' cargo-handling equipment by throwing it in the dock. One incident involved an assault on a docker who had accepted work to discharge a vessel from an employer who paid the union rate but was outside the ring of employers that organized the wreckers. The docker in question was frogmarched to the vessel, thrown down the gangway and ended up the local infirmary with contused ribs. It was incidents such as this that caused the dockers to turn their backs on the TGWU and take part in unofficial strike action to achieve their aims.

UNION RIVALRY: THE 'WHITES' VS THE 'BLUES'

During the 1950s the position of the TGWU was further weakened, particularly in the large northern ports. This occurred in August 1954 on the back of the 'Filling Strike' at Hull. The strike was triggered by a labour shortage on the Hull docks. To offset the shortage dockers from Cardiff had been brought to Hull under the terms of the National Dock Labour Scheme (see Chapter 8). In this instance twelve of the Cardiff men, who had been assigned to the port's King George Dock to discharge grain from a vessel named *The Seaboard Enterprise*, were expected to unload the grain via an outdated method known as bag-filling or hand-scuttling. This involved the arduous shovelling of grain into bags and bushels using metal scoops (see Chapter 4), a method that had been abolished in Cardiff some years previous. Attempts were made to transfer or 'shanghai' Hull men onto the job but, having seen their counterparts from Cardiff refuse the work, a port-wide strike ensued. However, the action was not backed by the TGWU's

4,000 DOCKERS STRIKE AT HULL

FOUR thousand Hull dockers stopped work to-day, and all the docks in the port were affected. Although addressed by their trade union leaders, the strikers refused to return to work.

A spokesman for the National Dock Labour Board told a reporter: "The port is completely idle. Every type of cargo is held up, including fruit as well as our main merchandise, which is grain."

The stoppage occurred at a time when shipping was at its peak at the port. Surplus labour from the ports of Cardiff and Swansea, as well as men from Goole, had been drafted into the port to alleviate the position.

The trouble began yesterday when 12 of the Cardiff dockers were allocated to the s.s Seaboard Enterprise (7,190 tons) to assist in unloading a cargo of grain. The ship was not at a silo berth, and the Cardiff men objected to the bag-filling system which was in operation. Their places were filled by Hull dockers, but they, too, stopped work.

When he addressed the dockers to-day Mr. J. Parnell, of the Transport and General Workers' Union, urged the men to return to work, but he was told by the men that they would remain out until the bag-filling system was abolished altogether.

The 1954 'filling strike' at Hull triggered the arrival of the London-based National Amalgamated Stevedores and Dockers' Union in the large northern ports. Hartlepool Mail, *17 August 1954.*

officials in the port, despite its unanimous support from the union's membership.

The action took a dramatic turn when the unofficial strike committee invited officials of the London-based National Amalgamated Stevedores and Dockers' Union (NASDU) to the port. NASDU, otherwise known as the 'Blue Union' due to its blue membership cards (the TGWU issued white cards), was not a new union. It was, in fact, a descendent of the aforementioned Labour Protection League which had established in London in 1872. Within forty-eight hours of the strike a vote of no confidence in the TGWU was passed. NASDU established new branches at Hull as well as Liverpool and Manchester and thousands of dockers left the TGWU and joined the 'Blues', whose overall membership swelled from 6,354 to 14,383. From there on a bitter rivalry between the 'Whites' and the 'Blues' began that was not eased until far-reaching reforms in the TGWU around a decade later (see Chapter 9).

Before I come on the dock I had a cousin who was quite a bit older than me called Jimmy Murphy and I think he was one of the instigators of bringing the Blue Union into Hull and eventually he got kicked off the dock I think that was one of the reason but another reason I was told . . . cos pre-war they had what they call a wreckers gang on the dock and this was a gang of men who was employed – this is only hearsay and they used to work for the employers and if anyone used try and break into the employers ring and you'd find the gear kicked in the dock the next day and I think it even went as far as men being threatened but I know there was an old bloke that I used to have drink with and had been a pre-war foreman and he worked for this particular firm who wasn't in the ring and he was the foreman for 'em and he said 'we had all our – we got to work the following morning and all our gear was kicked in the dock' and I think Jim, me cousin, was naming people who'd been in this ring and one or two was quite high officials in the White Union and I think it got to where he got something or other cos I was quite young then, I was still at school. But he got kicked off the dock but when I mentioned his name when I went on the dock I mentioned it to a few of the older dockers, he was quite well liked. So I think there was a little bit of skulduggery gone on there over that incident.

Some of the lads who came on with me their Dads had been in the Blue Union. I know a mate of mine, he joined both of them – he joined both! [Laughs] – There was little bit of rivalry I suppose you could say between the two unions it was a London union really . . . before I came on the dock it came in the 50s and so there was always that little bit of rivalry between the two unions but mostly the men got on OK . . . and you'd work alongside of each other no problem and I mean you'd agree with some of the things of the aspect of the Blue Union but I just stuck the White Union. But I had one Uncle who was in the Blue Union and one who was in the White and the White Union man was a really staunch union man and there was a little bit of friction between those two like.

THE RECORDS
Modern Records Centre (University of Warwick)
University Library, University of Warwick, Coventry, CV4 7AL
Tel: 024 7652 4219
Email: archives@warwick.ac.uk
Web: www.warwick.ac.uk/services/library/mrc
Online catalogue: http://mrc-catalogue.warwick.ac.uk/

The Modern Records Centre (MRC), founded in October 1973, is the main British repository for the archives of British trade unions and employers' organizations. Prior written permission in is required to view almost all unpublished records, which can be located on the Centre's. The archive of the Dock, Wharf, Riverside and General Workers' Union of Great Britain and Ireland, 1889–1922 is held here and contains some useful examples of paperwork held by members. The vast collection of records of the TGWU, 1920–2008, are also housed at the centre, including the Docks Group, which was one of the largest groups and sectors for most of the TGWU's existence. It must be noted that the collection does not include records of individual members, but it is incredibly useful for general information on the union and its officials. A guide to these records is on the centre's website: https://warwick.ac.uk/services/library/mrc/explorefurther/subject _guides/tgwu/.

The archive of the National Amalgamated Stevedores and Dockers' Union, 1880–1982 is also available. Of particular interest to family historians is the membership section of this collection. The Contribution Books give details of quarterly contributions made by the union's members, whilst the Accident Compensation Book, covering the years 1899 to 1921, offers details of accidents suffered by members alongside compensation received. The personal records of influential trade union leaders including Jack Jones (1898–2003) and Ben Tillett (1875–1943) and Ernest Bevin (1884–1951) are also archived at the MRC.

Hull History Centre
Worship St, Hull, HU2 8BG
Tel: 01482 317500
Email: hullhistorycentre@hcandl.co.uk
Web: www.hullhistorycentre.org.uk
Online catalogue: http://catalogue.hullhistorycentre.org.uk/.

Records of the TGWU, Region 10: Docks and Waterways, 1951-1990 (U DTG) are held at the Hull History Centre. Region 10 of the TGWU covered mainly Hull and Goole. Unfortunately, the records do not go back much beyond the early 1960s, and they are therefore most useful for studying the 1970s and 1980s. It is not known what happened to earlier records dating back to 1922. It must be noted that some of the records in this collection contain sensitive personal information and are therefore not open to the public, in accordance with the Freedom of Information Act (2000). For more information on the documents contained within this collection see http://catalogue.hullhistorycentre.org.uk/files/u-dtg.pdf.

The centre also holds the large record collection of the academic and writer Tony Topham (1881–1985) (U DTO). Topham was one of the leading figures among a group of academics and trade union leaders who, in the 1960s and 1970s, sought to advance the movement for workers' control in British industry. A

Yorkshireman born in Hull, Topham's whole life was centred around the cares and concerns of the dockers of Humberside, for whom he ran day-release educational classes on trade unionism. The papers relating to these courses are contained with the collection U DTO/1/54-58, as are materials relating to the docks industry, covering 1947–83, including files of newspaper cuttings relating to decasualisation, health and safety, containerisation, changes in cargo-handling and the TGWU (U DTO/1/41-50). There is also a statement on working conditions in Hull. More information about Tony Topham and the contents of this collection can be attained by visiting: http://catalogue.hullhistory centre.org.uk/files/u-dto.pdf.

Teeside Archives

Exchange, 6 Marton Road, Exchange Square, Middlesbrough, TS1 1DB
Tel: 01642 248321
Email: teessidearchives@middlesbrough.gov.uk
Online Catalogue: http://teessidearchives.middlesbrough.gov.uk/calmview/

The Tees Archives hold a large collection of TGWU records for the Tees region, including the Port of Middlesbrough. The majority of the records in this collection are largely administrative, but the following records offer an insight into wages, agreements and conditions: Tees Wharf Workers' Rates of Wages, 1936 and 1937 (U/TGW/3-4); Middlesbrough Dock Working Agreement, 1949 (U/TGW/16); Piece Rates, Manning Scales and General Conditions of Employment Applicable to Middlesbrough Dock Stevedores, 1953 (U/TGW/24); Agreement relating to Tippers on Iron Ore Wharves Dust Awards, 1955 (U/TGW/25).

Falkirk Archives
Callendar House, Callendar Park, Falkirk, FK1 1YR
Tel: 01324 503779
Email: archives@falkirkcommunitytrust.org
Web: www.falkirkcommunitytrust.org/heritage/archives/

Falkirk Archives hold the records of the Grangemouth Branch of the National Union of Dock Labourers and Riverside Workers (A1120). This archive contains an extensive collection of the union's minutes 1910–1960s, which include membership lists for 1933 to 1934 (A1120.011), but the best source for genealogists is the union's membership registers, covering 1908-69. It must be noted that the registers from around 1951 are currently closed under Data Protection laws. A useful guide to this collection is available to use at www.falkirkcommunitytrust.org/heritage/archives/finding-aids/docs/organizations/National_Union_of_ Dock _Labourers.pdf.

TRADE UNION OBJECTS: BANNERS AND BADGES
Banners formed an important part of the visual culture of the labour movement on the docks. Used during demonstrations and strikes, banners were commonly made from woven silk and adorned with colourful and dramatic oil-painted images and slogans that were based on themes of struggle, charity, solidarity and labour: 'Let all men work for each mans good and live in noble brotherhood', 'Union and Victory', 'Never friendless' and 'Justice to the toilers'. Badges, like banners, were also colourful symbols of union pride. The first trade union badges can be traced back to the 1830s, but it was the establishment of the Dock, Wharf, Riverside and General Workers' Union in 1889 that saw union badges increasingly issued to union members on the docks. A useful site for those wishing to learn more about the badges of the dockers' unions is: www.unionbadges.wordpress. com. For

museum collections on the docks unions visit the following two museums:

People's History Museum (Manchester)

Left Bank, Spinningfields, Manchester, M3 3ER
Tel: 0161 838 9190
Email: info@phm.org.uk
Web: www.phm.org.uk

Manchester's People's History Museum is the National Museum for Democracy. The museum is housed in two galleries. In Main Gallery One is a section entitled Workers, which explores the origins and history of trade unionism, and includes an exhibit that contains items and information relating to waterfront unionism. In addition, the museum's online collection provides an excellent display of other objects relating to the dockers unions including banners, badges, photographs and ephemera: http://www.phm.org.uk/keemu/

The People's Story Museum (Edinburgh)

163 Canongate, Edinburgh, EH8 8BN
Tel: 0131 529 4057
Email: MuseumsAndGalleries@edinburgh.gov.uk
Web: www.edinburghmuseums.org.uk/venue/peoples-story-museum

The collections of the People's Story Museum in Edinburgh focuses on the history, culture, crafts and trades of the city's people, this includes the Leith Dockers. The museum features a display relating to the dockers as well as other items including banners and flags of the Leith Dockers' Union, tools, documents such as rate agreements and a few papers such as letters of reference from the docks, as well as some photographs. Art works depicting the docks are also held by the museum.

RECOMMENDED READS

A large body of work on the history of trade unionism has been completed. The following highlights the best reads relating to collective action on the docks. Not surprisingly there are a number of books about the Great Dock Strike of 1889; amongst the best are Terry McCarthy's *The Great Dock Strike, 1889* (Weidenfeld & Nicolson, 1988) and *The Great Dock Strike, 1889* (London: Longman, 1974) by David Wasp and Alan Davis.

There are several good books available regarding the early development of trade unionism at particular ports. For London see *Dock, Wharf, Riverside and General Workers' Union: A Brief History of the Dockers Union, Commemorating the 1889 Dock Strike* (Twentieth Century Press, 1910) by Ben Tillett, and John Lovell's *Stevedores and Dockers: A Study of Trade Unionism in the Port of London, 1870-1914* (MacMillan, 1969); early Liverpool unionism is the focus of *Liverpool Dockers and Seamen 1870-1890* (University of Hull Publications, 1974) and *The Dockers' Union: A Study of the National Union of Dock Labourers, 1889-1922* (Leicester University Press, 1985), both by Eric Taplin; William Kenefick's '*Rebellious and Contrary': The Glasgow Dockers, 1853–1932* (Tuckwell Press, 2000) is essential for reading for Glasgow and Clydeside; Those interested in Hull should read *Waterfront Organization in Hull, 1870-1900* (University of Hull Publications, 1972) by Raymond Brown and Keith Brooker's *The Hull Strikes of 1911* (East Yorkshire Local History Society, 1979).

The best publication on the dockers' unofficial industrial action after the Second World War is William 'Bill' Hunter's *They Knew Why They Fought: Unofficial Struggles and Leadership on the Docks 1945-1989* (Index Books, 1994). There are two good short studies that give detailed insights into the events surrounding the arrival of the 'Blue Union' in the northern ports; John Archer's *The Struggle for an Independent Trade Union by the Dockers in Merseyside and Hull during 1954-1955* (1995) and *How the Blue Union came to Hull Docks* (1995) by Keith Sinclair.

Chapter 6

BEYOND THE DOCK WALL: DOCKSIDE COMMUNITIES

As previous chapters have shown, the origins, working practices and organization of dock workers made them one of the most distinctive and tight-knit labour groups in the country. Confined to their work territories on the docks and suspicious of outsiders, the dockers were often viewed as a race apart by the rest of society. This perception was further reinforced by the dockers' habits outside of the workplace, including their tendencies to live in exclusive neighbourhoods close to the dock gates and their congregation in the dockside pubs. Features of the dockers' community on the other side of the dock wall form the content of this chapter which also shows how researchers can find out more about the social and family lives of their ancestors.

DOCKSIDE NEIGHBOURHOODS
Chapter 2 established how the navvies, who dug out the docks in the nineteenth and early twentieth centuries, often settled in neighbourhoods closeby and stayed on to work the docks they had helped to dig. With dock work passed strictly from father to son, the descendents of the navvies continued to reside close to the dock gates into the twentieth century. Housing in such areas was generally poor, cramped and overpopulated by large families. Dockside neighbourhoods were often situated close to warehouses, goods yards and maritime industries such as

shipbuilding and repair yards or mills, factories and yards that processed seaborne goods such as cotton, oil seeds, grain, cow hides or timber.

Dockside communities generally became less concentrated during the twentieth century. The interwar years saw slum clearance schemes in port cities that caused docking families to be relocated to newly-built housing often away from the waterfront. Dockside communities were further fragmented by the severe bomb damage suffered by many British ports (see Chapter 7) and the further construction of new housing in the 1950s and 1960s. Nevertheless, a strong sense of community pervaded in surviving dockside neighbourhoods as well as the new housing estates where dockers would congregate in the pubs and working men's clubs where they lived.

LEISURE AND RECREATION

Hard work was often coupled with hard drinking amongst the dockers who would congregate in the many dockside pubs and taverns. Like other working class groups dockers keenly attended spectator sports. In Hull Rugby League was the sport of choice with Hull Kingston Rovers (established in 1882) known as a dockers' team. Almost everywhere else, however, it was football that attracted the dockers during their leisure time. Millwall F.C., established in 1885, has its roots in the East End at Millwall docks on the Isle of Dogs, although the club relocated to Bermondsey on the South Bank of the Thames in 1910. Before becoming known as the Lions, the club's nickname was originally the Dockers. The club's association with dock workers continues to be strong today. In recent years Millwall has celebrated its links with London's docks by introducing 'Dockers' Days', and archiving the club's dock roots in the Millwall FC Museum. Furthermore, in 2011, the club officially named the east stand of their stadium as the 'Dockers Stand' in honour of the club's former nickname. Millwall and West Ham United, the latter

A large group of dockers on an evening out c. 1950s. A tight-knit community, dockers often sought out the company of their co-workers outside of work.

traditionally being the club of the East End dockers, share a bitter rivalry, with matches between the two teams known as the 'dockers' derby'.

> Oh they used to go to the pubs pretty regularly [Laughs]. Not me. There was a clan that used to go at 11 o'clock – 'are you alright lad? … are you alright? Can you manage there? – just going to have a quick drink' and they used to go and they used to come back at 3 o'clock.

WOMEN AND CHILDREN ON THE WATERFRONT

Whilst the docks were undoubtedly a male-dominated environment, women shared the hardship and privations of the dockers. The wives and women who were reliant on the dockers lived with financial insecurity and the constant fear that their spouse would be injured, maimed or even killed on the docks. Womens' health also suffered as a result of their men working with insanitary and toxic cargoes. In recent years many dockers' wives have been diagnosed with respiratory illnesses contracted from toxic cargoes like asbestos to which they were exposed when washing their husband's clothes decades ago.

Women were involved in work on the docks indirectly. Many worked in the dockside cafes mentioned in Chapter 3, which served the dockers with the hearty food they required. Others were involved in clerical work with stevedoring firms, merchants and port authorities that employed dockers. Following the introduction of the National Dock Labour Scheme in 1947, women worked as state registered nurses at the Labour Board's medical centres on the docks, tending to the many injuries sustained by dock labourers in the course of their work. They also staffed the Board's newly-established dockside canteens from the 1970s (see Chapter 8).

The wife of one docker recollected:

The men used to go out, they used to have to be there before eight o'clock to get a job. What the women used to do, they used to stand at the top of the terrace and watch the men coming home and they'd say: 'Oh Albert hasn't got a job' or 'Ted hasn't got a job', 'Bill hasn't got job'. Then they'd turn to me mother and say: 'Ooh, Chuck must be working'. They used to get 12 shillings and six pence a day. On the night me dad would give me mother 12 and six and she would put the rent and insurance and all the payments on the mantelpiece. She said 'Oh, that's good, he'll get 12 and six tonight'. Well all these women had no money for their dinner, so what she did, she went and lent them all half a crown and she took half a crown and she went and got a rabbit and veggies. So she gets this rabbit all ready to put in the oven, and sure enough Chuck come walking down the street. He'd been dawdling. So she gets this rabbit and she says: 'You can't have it! I thought you were working! You can't have it! Oh, what am I going to do for my rent?' she's loaned all her money out so the women in the terrace could get a dinner in!

The wife of another docker describes how:

> Well I've got the asbestosis off him – washing his clothes – asbestos plaques and then if he was on that and he was on two or three days I used to say to him 'how long will you be on it?' and he had a rough idea how much was in the hold and what had to come out and he'd say 'well I'll be on it three days' and we'd just give his clothes a good shake and then put 'em on – you couldn't bring 'em in the house, couldn't bring 'em in the house they had to go in an out cupboard. I knew he'd worked among it, you see it [asbestosis] doesn't show up for years and some men had worked on it . . . cos he used to come home covered in it as if . . . you know when you've worked on flour? Real fine powder and of course I used to shake his things and wash 'em apparently there's quite a few wives with it.'

Children, like their parents, experienced poverty and hardship in dockside neighbourhoods, yet growing up in streets around the docks was often exciting. Some of the older docks in port towns were open and children would often play on and around the sheds and cargo. However, most docks were enclosed behind high walls and were a source of mystery and intrigue to children who could only see the tops of quayside cranes and ships' funnels against the skyline. In Liverpool, children would rattle off the names of the numerous docks like a skipping rhyme – 'Clarence, Langton, Huskisson, North Canada, South Canada'. Dockers would often bring their children exotic goods acquired from foreign sailors such as fruit or pets like parrots and monkeys.

Children in a dockside neighbourhood c. 1910.

The daughter of a docker recalled:

I remember on a Friday before dad came home, we used to have to have crisps and banana sandwiches for tea until dad came home with his wages cos sometimes . . . I can't remember what day it was and I used to have to go to the little shop at the end of the street and get a banana and a packet of crisps with a twist of salt in . . . cos we'd run out of money and we had rent to pay and everything out of [dad's wages].

Childhood memories of growing up close to the Goole docks:

> The street I lived in, there was house on that side and that side of the street it was sheds – dock sheds that went onto the dock and me father his barge was tied up. Especially during the war years leading up to the invasion – the Normandy invasion there was a lot of what they call ducks – an amphibious thing what the army used on the beach and they could drive – they was lined up in the street outside the houses ready to go. So as a little lad I'd climb on them and the shed at the bottom of the street there was crates of lorries all in bits ready to be crated up and we used to be climbing in and out of them so for a little kid of six it was a wonderland. I remember I took me little mate on the dock to play on my Dad's – it was a barge then and my Dad found out and you can imagine what happened then – all playing on the dock. I did fall in when I was little but my Dad pulled me out.

POVERTY

Unemployment and a lack of financial security were constant evils of the casual system, especially before the introduction of the registration schemes (see Chapter 5). Dockers, therefore, were exposed to poverty and hardship more than most other occupations. Most dockside areas were poor and often little more than slums, this was largely due to irregular wages and poor pay. This excerpt from 'Labour and the Poor' by Henry Mayhew in the *Morning Chronicle* from 26 October 1849, gives an idea of the condition of the neighbourhoods near London's docks:

> The courts and alleyways round about the Dock swarm with low lodging-houses and are inhabited either by the dock labourers, sack-makers, watermen or that peculiar class of London poor who pick up a precarious living by the

waterside. The open streets themselves have all, more or less, a maritime character. Every other shop is either stocked with gear for the ship or for the sailor. The windows of one house are filled with quadrants and bright brass sextants, chronometers and huge mariner's compasses, with their cards trembling with the motion of the carts and wagons passing in the street.

Those dock labourers who could not find alternative work when trade slumps hit the docks found themselves and their family reliant on the Poor Law. From 1834 the poor were housed in workhouses where they would be clothed and fed. Children who entered the workhouse would receive some schooling. In return for this care, all workhouse paupers would have to work for several hours each day.

CRIME

Other dockers turned to crime during times of unemployment or to supplement their meagre wages. Prior to the introduction of containers and other unitised cargo-handling methods in the 1960s, goods would pass openly between ships' holds and the quays, warehouses and yards of docklands. Unsurprisingly, not all goods reached their intended destination. The true nature of theft on the docks has always been a matter of dispute. Few dockers would have denied that a certain amount of pilfering did take place, but the owners of missing merchandise would probably have spoken of extensive networks through which large quantities of stolen goods were stored and fenced.

A former docks policeman remembered:

When you go into sheds and such-like you will observe various things of what cargo is in there and everything else and this guy came walking down – walking down the slope to the Dock towards me and I thought 'they're a pair of shoes that we've got in the sheds' so I stopped him 'where you got your pair of shoes from?' he said 'I got 'em from a company down the Road' so I said 'what did yer pay for it? Blah, blah, blah. Right I'm arresting you on suspicion of theft' you see went down to this place he'd said 'well I've never sold 'em but I'd like to know where you get 'em from, they're good quality!' and from that he'd got stuff at home he'd stolen and I got a commendation from the Magistrates on that one for me observation and such like. We used to deal with all offences that the outside forces would deal with.

The wife of one docker living in a dockside neighbourhood recalled:

There used to be a lot of pilfering and middle of the night one night this light came across the window and I thought, what's going on out there? And I looked out and there's two Policemen – dock Policemen and we went downstairs and opened the door and 'Mrs Cooke?' 'Yeah' and 'can we come and see . . . what you've got?' and somebody had been stealing raw alcohol but it wasn't George Cooke it was Tommy Cook! This was in the middle of the night and then they came again the next morning and they looked in all my cupboards see if we had any of this raw alcohol . . . some of em had been very ill they'd been in hospital with it . . . drinking raw . . . ethanol. Another problem living close to the docks was foreign seamen going

BELFAST DOCKER JAILED

Receiving charge

A Belfast dock labourer was sentenced to one month's imprisonment at Belfast Custody Court yesterday for receiving 3½ lb. of confectionery, valued at 12s. the property of Burns Laird Shipping Lines.

He was Robert John Bell (51), of Westmoreland Street. He pleaded guilty.

Harbour Constable R. H. Keenan said that he saw Bell coming from the Glasgow shed at Donegall Quay and twice going to a car parked at Albert Square. In the dashboard of the car he (witness) found the confectionery.

Bell, who was stated to have had a previous conviction in 1948, said that he had not been in trouble since then.

Crime, particularly theft, was often associated with the docks. Belfast News-Letter, *2 July 1955.*

to the ladies who offered them services [laughs] two of 'em walked in my house and my daughter was in the bath in front of the fire as a baby just opened the door and walked in they'd got the wrong house. Cos we were so close to the docks, I remember 'em going to another house once and digging the garden up cos stuff had been nicked off the dock and they turned up and dug all the beds up.'

THE RECORDS

Oral History: The richest source of information about households and docking communities are contained in the memories, reminiscences and stories of the men, women and children who lived and worked on the waterfront. Whilst censuses document who was living where and with whom at a single point in history, they offer little, if any, insight, into family life, relationships and culture in dockside neighbourhoods. The memories of our older relatives are not just limited to their own lifetime. We inherit the memories of our parents and grandparents through stories and anecdotes. Consequently, dock workers may tell us about the memories and experiences passed on from their forebears who also laboured on the docks.

Recording interviews with living docker relatives and their families is very useful as researchers can refer back to recorded memories and stories as research progresses. Furthermore, it is an excellent way of preserving family history for future generations. With permission from the interviewee, interviews can easily be recorded on devices such as mobile phones and dictaphones. Remembering is not always easy, especially when trying to recall events that occurred many years ago. However, objects such as old photographs, maps or newspaper cuttings can provide excellent prompts. If family members are willing and able, walking interviews around old haunts is also a good way of stimulating memories.

Some oral history work has been completed with dockers. The book *Voices of Leith Dockers* (Mercat Press, 2001) by Ian MacDougal is by far the most comprehensive collection of published oral histories. In 2009 Glasgow Museums conducted an oral history project with local dockers entitled 'Quay Voices'. The transcripts and recordings can be accessed by appointment at:

Glasgow Museums Resource Centre
200 Woodhead Road, Glasgow, G53 7NN
Email: navigator@glasgowlife.org.uk
Tel: 0141 276 9300
Web: www.glasgowlife.org.uk/museums/venues/glasgow-museums
-resource-centre-gmrc

Bristol's Floating Harbour Museum also has an excellent collection of oral history interviews gathered over the last forty years. Many recordings are of dockers, seamen and families that lived close to the Harbour. They give a tremendous flavour of life in the Harbour when it was a commercial port. Some of the audio and transcripts are available on the museum's website: www.bristolfloatingharbour.org.uk/oral-history/.

UK Census Returns (see Chapter 1): available every decade 1841–1911. are valuable for learning about docking households and neighbourhoods. The census returns record the name, age and occupation of residents in each household, from 1851 onwards details of place of birth, marital status and the relationship to the head of the household are included.

Newspapers (see Chapter 1): offer some insight into the nature of theft on the docks, the culprits and the fate of the goods that made their way illicitly beyond the dock wall.

Workhouse Records: After 1834 parishes were grouped into Poor Law Unions each run by a board of guardians elected by ratepayers from their constituent parishes. The daily management of the workhouse was supervised by a workhouse master and a matron. The day-to-day administrative records of the workhouses can be found in local archives. A comprehensive list of archives holding workhouse and poor law records can be found on www.workhouses.org.uk/records/archives; an excellent website that contains much information on the workhouses. The records held at local archives commonly include:

- Admission and discharge registers.
- Birth, baptism, creed and death registers.
- Inmate and out relief lists.

Some Poor Law and workhouse records for port areas are available on line. On Ancestry (see Chapter 1) are the London Workhouse Admission and Discharge Records, 1659–1930 and the London Poor Law and Board of Guardian Records, 1430–1930. On Findmypast (see Chapter 1) are the Manchester Workhouse admission and discharge registers, 1800–1911, whilst the deaths of those who died in the Runcorn Poor Law Union can be found in the Cheshire Workhouse records.

Chapter 7

DOCKS AND DOCKERS DURING THE WORLD WARS

British ships carrying seaborne trade were the nation's lifeline during both World Wars. Consequently, the ports and their dockers were vital to the war effort. This was recognized by the government which took innovative measures to ensure a ready supply of labour on the docks in both conflicts. The importance of the ports made them natural targets for the enemy who wrought death and destruction on the waterfront. Indeed, port

A tank being lowered into the hold of a ship during the Second World War.

cities became front-line cities. In the First World War there was the new and terrifying threat of Zeppelins, which dropped bombs on the docks and their adjacent neighbourhoods where many dockers resided (see Chapter 6). Technological advances in aerial warfare during the interwar period meant that, during the Second World War, the ports and their people were subjected to a more sophisticated threat in the form of the Luftwaffe. This chapter provides details of the organization and work of dock labourers in each of the world wars as well as the bombardment experienced by dockers and their families. Each section also contains information on where to locate war-related documents including military records.

THE FIRST WORLD WAR, 1914–1918
Dockers in Khaki: First Dock Battalion of the Liverpool Regiment

When Great Britain declared war on Germany on 4 August 1914 thousands of dockers, like many other members of the working classes, volunteered for military service. This left a severe shortage of labour on the docks. Realizing that the dockers were vital to the war effort as they were required to move essential goods, the Government exempted dock workers from military service. The early part of the war saw much congestion of shipping at London but also at Liverpool where much shipping traffic had been diverted from Southampton and the east coast ports. Some 8,000 dockers from Merseyside docks had volunteered for service between August 1914 and January 1915 and congestion on the estuary was particularly acute. In the early part of 1915 as many as forty-four steamships were awaiting berths at Liverpool, with some vessels having waited for over a month to be discharged. Congestion in the port's warehouses and on the railways, coupled with the occasional shortage of carts, caused goods and merchandise to become stacked on the quaysides near berths, which caused added problems and delays. A shortage of dock labour and the casual system were identified as key to the problems at Liverpool. Whilst many experienced dockers had volunteered, the men that remained could often earn their weekly wage within a few days from widely-available overtime and then take the rest of the week off. The casual system that had favoured employers before the war now worked to the advantage of the dockers.

The labour situation in the port encouraged the War Office to authorize Lord Derby on 29 March 1915 to raise a battalion of dock labourers to work the Merseyside docks. Styled the 'First Dock Battalion' of the Liverpool Regiment, the dockers were to primarily handle important Government cargoes but could also be hired out to employers. The battalion was issued with khaki overalls from which they acquired the nickname of 'Khaki dockers'. The Government guaranteed the workers a minimum wage of 35 shillings a week for the loading and unloading of war supplies. By July 1915 the Battalion numbered around 1,100 men, but in December a second battalion was formed and by May 1917 the force reached 1,750. Serving in the Battalion did not exempt the men from front-line service and fifty-three men were sent to combat units during December 1917 and January 1918.

ENROLLING THE DOCKERS.

MEASURES TO KEEP THE SOLDIERS SUPPLIED.

FULL SCHEME.

BATTALION OF WORKERS ON ARMY SERVICE.

A STRIKING STEP.

Liverpool dockers enrolling in the First Dock Battalion of the Liverpool Regiment. Liverpool Echo, *31 March 1915.*

The creation and operation of the Docks Battalion attracted great interest in a number of ports outside of Liverpool. Leading figures in the ports of Glasgow, Greenock, Hull, Fleetwood and Manchester all made enquiries to the Battalion on solutions to the congestion of shipping traffic via the organization of dock labour. Furthermore, the General Manager of the Cardiff Railway Company contemplated the creation of a 'Bute Docks Battalion of Dock Workers' based on the Liverpool model, although this was rejected by the War Office. The Docks Battalion never replaced the civilian organization of dockers in Liverpool during the War, but its creation and operation was an important experiment in the military organization of industrial labour.

The First Blitz: 'Zeppelin Raids' on the Ports

Aerial attacks on British ports and industrial targets are associated with the Second World War, yet the First World War saw the country's docklands become the target of enemy bombardment. During the conflict several port cities suffered bombing and incendiary raids by Zeppelins and Schütte-Lanz rigid airships. Such attacks, generally referred to as 'Zeppelin raids', were a terrifying experience for British civilians who had largely been unaffected by war prior to the twentieth century. Blackouts and evacuations were of the most basic kind and, despite being warned of the raid hours in advance, there was little people could do except wait for the bombs to fall from the airships.

The first Zeppelin raid in January 1915 was directed at the Humber Estuary with its ports and industries at Grimsby, Immingham, Hull and Goole. However, strong winds caused the Zeppelins to divert their attack to Great Yarmouth and the port town of King's Lynn. The raid cost nine lives as well as damage to buildings some of which were close to the docks.

A German Imperial Order dated 12 February 1915 authorized the bombing of London's docks, although the first attempts failed due to bad weather. Over the following year London suffered several raids with dockside areas badly affected. In the first raid on the capital on 31 May Stepney was hit in an attack where a total of 120 bombs were dropped, which killed seven people, injured thirty-five and started forty-one fires. A further raid by two Zeppelins over 7 and 8 September caused damage across the Isle of Dogs, Deptford, Bermondsey and Rotherhithe.

London was the intended target of another raid in June 1915, but bad weather caused the attack to be diverted to Hull, which was hit by thirteen explosive and fifty incendiary bombs, destroying forty houses and killing twenty-four people. Hull suffered several raids during the war, although the city avoided one particular raid when the nearby port of Goole was mistaken for Hull. On 31 March 1916, five Zeppelins set out to attack London and East Anglia, but as Zeppelin *L22* approached England, it developed engine problems, so instead of heading for London changed course for Grimsby docks. Bombs were dropped but landed harmlessly in open countryside close to the nearby seaside resort of Cleethorpes. A second attack, however, saw Cleethorpes hit, with twenty-seven people dying instantly and four fatally injured, dying soon after from their wounds.

Smaller ports were also targeted by the Zeppelins. In April 1916 a raid on Leith and Edinburgh killed ten, including three children, and seriously injured several others. There were also three Zeppelin raids on the Hartlepools. The second raid on 27 November 1916 took place over West Hartlepool with bombs damaging many shops and houses inland to the west of the West Hartlepool docks. During 1917 the Zeppelin raids were largely replaced by aeroplane attacks. By the time of the Armistice on 11 November 1918 there had been a total of 52 airship raids on Britain that claimed the lives of more than 500 people and 1,358 injured, many of whom resided in port towns and cities.

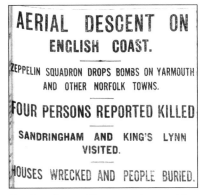

AERIAL DESCENT ON ENGLISH COAST.

ZEPPELIN SQUADRON DROPS BOMBS ON YARMOUTH AND OTHER NORFOLK TOWNS.

FOUR PERSONS REPORTED KILLED

SANDRINGHAM AND KING'S LYNN VISITED.

HOUSES WRECKED AND PEOPLE BURIED.

During the conflict several port cities suffered bombing and incendiary raids by Zeppelins and Schütte-Lanz airships. Daily Record, *20 January 1915.*

The Records

Military Records: The service records of British dockers who enlisted in the military and the Docks Battalions of the Liverpool Regiment are available on Ancestry and Findmypast (see Chapter 1) in the respective British Army WWI Service Records, 1914–1920 sections. These records contain a variety of forms, including:

- Attestation forms (the form completed by the individual on enlistment).
- Medical history forms.
- Casualty forms.
- Disability statements.
- Regimental conduct sheets.
- Awards.
- Proceedings on Discharge.
- Cover for Discharge Documents.
- Index Cards.

The type of information contained in these records includes: name of solider, age, birthplace, occupation, marital status, regiment number, date of attestation and physical description. Both sites also include any other useful military records including British Army WWI Medal Rolls Index Cards, 1914-1920. Findmypast also offers www.livesofthefirstworldwar.org which forms the Imperial War Museum's permanent digital memorial. Here you can view and upload photos, information and stories of your First World War ancestor and connect with other researchers. The site also has access to over 300 million military and civilian records. Many features and records on the site are free but some require a monthly subscription. Those wishing to trace the military graves of their fallen ancestors both home and overseas can do so for free on the Commonwealth War Graves Commission (CWGC) website www.cwgc.org.

Newspapers (see Chapter 1): Local, regional and national newspapers contain numerous detailed articles and images relating to the docks and dockers during the First World War. These include the raising of the Docks Battalion at Liverpool, the Zeppelin raids discussed in this chapter, and episodes of industrial unrest that occurred in various ports around the country during the war.

On Film: Some short pieces of British Pathé archival film relating to dock workers and the First World War are available to view at www.britishpathe.com. The films include one of Private William Ratcliffe, a Liverpudlian docker of the South Lancashire Regiment, who was awarded the Victoria Cross in 1917 (Film IDs: 1872.13, 1890.34 and 1359.09). There is also footage of members of the Docks Battalion of the Liverpool Regiment marching in army uniforms through the streets of Liverpool (Film ID: 1912.11)

THE SECOND WORLD WAR
The Wartime Dock Labour Schemes

At the start of the Second World War the government recognized the paramount importance of ensuring a regular supply of dock labour for the movement of essential seaborne goods. One of the first initiatives to achieve this was made by the Minister of Labour Ernest Bevin in June 1940 under the Emergency Powers (Defence) Act. Bevin made the registration of all dockers and employers of dock labour compulsory, with the former being eligible for movement between the ports. Such was their importance to the war effort, the dockers were one of the first groups to be covered by registration alongside professional engineers, scientists, chemists, physicists and quantity surveyors.

Later in 1940 two schemes were formulated for the employment and maintenance of the dock labour force. The first was introduced by the Ministry of War Transport to cover the north-west ports including Liverpool, Birkenhead, Manchester,

Preston, Garston, Bromborough, Ellesmere Port, Partington, Widnes, Runcorn and Weston Point, and later the Clyde ports, where the vital Atlantic convoys were being handled. This scheme was controlled by two regional port directors (Merseyside and Clydeside) and ensured dockers would receive a guaranteed weekly wage of £4 2s 6d per week.

The second scheme was established by Bevin in September 1941 under the Essential Work (Dock Labour) Order and covered the remaining ports. Unlike the first scheme, the second was controlled by the newly-created National Dock Labour Corporation via a number of local boards. Both national and local boards were jointly administered by representatives of the employers of dock labour and the Transport and General Workers' Union; an interesting experiment in industrial democracy. By June 1941 the Corporation was employing almost 44,000 dock workers. The Corporation provided the basis for the post War National Dock Labour Scheme, which will be discussed in Chapter 8.

The Luftwaffe: Death and Destruction on the Waterfront

During the Second World War ports and dock workers were even more essential to securing victory than they had been in the Great War. Developments in aerial warfare meant that docklands and their industries could be more precisely targeted than they had been by the Zeppelins. Using airfields in occupied Norway, Holland, Belgium and France, the Luftwaffe wrought considerable damage to docklands. Across the ports, wharves, quays, warehouses, railway lines and industries considerable damage was sustained from enemy bombing. Whilst the dockers' places of work were damaged, many who resided in the streets and neighbourhoods close to the docks lost their lives, families and homes to enemy bombs.

Unsurprisingly, the greatest level of damage occurred in the Port of London where a third of all facilities were either damaged or destroyed. More than 25,000 bombs were dropped on the capital's docklands, many of which fell on the Royal Docks. Indeed, it was at the docks where the Blitz of the capital began on Saturday, 7 September 1940 when the city and port sustained a massive daylight raid. This was followed by ninety consecutive nights of night-time bombing. Incendiary bombs, designed to start fires quickly, were particularly effective as most dock warehouses had timber interiors that ignited easily. During the Blitz it is estimated that over 107,000 tonnes of shipping in the Thames was damaged. Nearby, in the East End, which was densely populated by many connected with docks and its associated transport and industries, 400 people were killed and 1,600 injured.

The greatest damage outside of London was sustained by Hull. Located on the east coast a short distance across the North Sea from occupied Holland and Belgium, the port and its industries suffered large-scale destruction. Every dock in the port sustained damage, with the south side of Albert Dock and the Riverside Quay being completely obliterated. At Victoria Dock, the port's principal timber-handling facility, huge fires also caused widespread damage to warehousing, quays and coal conveyors. Large-scale attacks took place on several nights in March 1941, resulting in some 200 deaths. However, the most concentrated attacks were between 3 and 9 May 1941, which resulted in 400 deaths. Another large-scale attack took place in July 1941 with around 140 fatalities. Many of those who lost their lives resided in the Hessle and Hedon Road areas located close to the docks. Indeed, Hull was so severely targeted that a secret department of the Air Ministry planned and constructed decoy docks on the Humber to the east of the city. Operational from around August 1941, the decoys successfully contributed towards limiting damage to the docks.

Ports on the West Coast were also attacked by the Luftwaffe. Liverpool, the country's main transatlantic convoy port during the war and a naval base for the Admiralty's entire Atlantic campaign from 1941, was also badly hit. The Port's Huskisson Branch Dock Number 2 was almost completely destroyed during a raid in May 1941 when the fully-loaded ammunition ship SS *Malakand* exploded. Requisitioned by the Admiralty for berthing corvettes, Albert Dock too suffered from bombing in May 1941, with the south-west stack badly damaged. Bristol also endured numerous air raids with German bombers targeting the docks at Avonmouth. The worst raid on the city was on 24 November 1940 when bombers dropped 1,540 tons of high explosives and 12,500 incendiaries. The raid left 207 dead and 187 seriously injured. On the south coast Southampton too was hit by heavy raids in November 1940, with one raid seeing 800 high-explosive bombs dropped.

Outside of England, Cardiff in South Wales was badly bombed on 2 January 1941. While the city's docks and factories were hit, residential areas also suffered. The attack on Cardiff caused the

A tank vital to the war effort being safely stowed.

Dockers engaged in war work.

deaths of 165 people as well as numerous injuries. Cardiff was again bombed over several nights in March of 1941. In Scotland it was the shipbuilding yards on the Clyde that were the principal targets of the enemy, but bombs also landed on the docks at Glasgow. Even Belfast in Northern Ireland sustained aerial attacks. This first occurred during April 1941, with the port's docks and shipyards being the primary target. As in other dockside cities, the residential areas nearby were also badly hit.

Wartime Work on the Docks
Alongside miners, farmers, scientists, merchant seaman and variety of other workers, dock workers were classed as belonging to a reserved occupation during the war. They were, therefore, exempt from military service. The emergency of war was not enough to ease industrial relations between dock labour and

employers on the home front, however. There were some thirty strikes in each of the war years, in spite of the Government Order 1305 which made strikes and lock-outs illegal pending arbitration by the Ministry of Labour. Furthermore, absenteeism had been an ongoing problem amongst dock workers as well as the tendency of some to walk off a job when the handling of other better-paying cargoes became available. At Liverpool absenteeism reached 30 per cent of the workforce at its peak and 13.5 per cent at London.

The dockers' wartime industrial action and absenteeism was, and has since been, condemned as selfish and unpatriotic by some sections of the media. Sadly, this has often overshadowed the vital war work undertaken by the dockers, which was often performed amidst the rubble of bomb damage and severe shortages. Throughout the war the dockers handled thousands of tons of valuable cargoes that fed the nation and contributed to the war effort. In addition, dock workers at a number of ports handled vital cargoes and military stores for major offensives including the Allied invasion of Italy and the D-Day landings.

The Records
Military Service Records: Military records for those dockers who were not registered under the wartime schemes are, like all service records, subject to 100 years' closure. However, it is possible to apply to view an ancestor's records via the relevant application forms, which can be downloaded from the Government's website at www.gov.uk/get-copy-military-service-records. Full records will be released to proven next of kin. Only very basic information about deceased service personnel will be released to other enquirers, with slightly more detail made available 25 years after the date of death. Furthermore, it must be noted that there is a fee involved (currently £30) and enquiries can take several months to process.

Records of the Wartime Dock Labour Schemes: The largest collection of records relating the wartime schemes and the registered dockers are held at The National Archives:

The National Archives
Kew, Richmond, Surrey, TW9 4DU
Tel: 020 8876 3444
Web: www.nationalarchives.gov.uk

The regional controllers of the Merseyside and Clydeside dock labour schemes can be found under archive reference MT63. Alternatively, the records of the National Dock Labour Corporation records and those of some of the local boards are under BK. More information on this collection can be found through The National Archives' online archive catalogue: http://discovery.nationalarchives.gov.uk/. Records relating to the Corporation and its local boards are discussed more extensively in Chapter 8.

Air Raid Records: The National Archives also holds a collection of records that are very useful for finding out information about air raids and bomb damage in ports, which newspapers censored from their reports. Relevant records include the 'Bomb Census Survey Records, 1940–1945', which are part of the Home Office archive (HO). In September 1940 the government started to collect and collate information relating to damage sustained during bombing raids. London and Liverpool were included in the early surveys, but by September 1941 the bomb census had been extended to cover the rest of the UK and included the rest of the country's ports. Its purpose was to provide the government with a complete picture of air raid patterns, types of weapon used and the damage caused – in particular to strategic services and installations such as transport infrastructure, including ports, and industry. The most insightful information is contained in HO192,

HO193 and HO198. Many records about air raids and bomb damage on the docks, such as 'Air Raid Incident Files' produced by Air Raid Wardens and the Police, are held at local and county archives.

The 1939 Register (see Chapter 1): As established in Chapter 1, the 1939 Register, available with a subscription to Findmypast or Ancestry, is an essential record for those wishing to find out more about their docker ancestors on the eve of the Second World War. The register records names, addresses, martial statuses, exact dates of birth, occupation and whether the individual was a member of the armed services or reserves.

Newspapers (see Chapter 1): Although heavily censored during the war, local, regional and national newspapers can still be useful to family historians as they contain occasional reports about strikes and enemy bombing on the docks.

On Film: 'Swansea Docks in the War Years' is a 17-minute piece of archive film available to view free on the British Film Institute's website: https://player.bfi.org.uk/free/film/watch-swansea-docks-in-the-war-years-1947-online. Despite the title, the film shows the bustling Swansea docks at the end of the war. A torpedoed ship is in for repair and a trawler arrives with fish, whilst biscuits for the hungry and displaced peoples of Europe are loaded by dockers.

Recommended Reads
Henry Bradford's *Dockers' Stories from the Second World War* (The History Press, 2011) offers a collection of several true wartime stories, drawn from the author's time as a docker in the Port of London.

Chapter 8

THE NATIONAL DOCK LABOUR SCHEME

It is impossible to appreciate the working lives of docker ancestors in the second half of the twentieth century without knowing something about the National Dock Labour Scheme. From its establishment in 1947 until its abolition in 1989 the scheme administered virtually every aspect of the dockers' daily lives, from their morning fight for work at the call to their evening and weekend socialising and recreation. This chapter describes the scheme's origins and purpose, its different facets and where to find the many records it generated.

THE ORIGINS AND CREATION OF THE SCHEME

The National Dock Labour Scheme (NDLS) was largely modelled on the wartime scheme that was controlled by the National Dock Labour Corporation (see Chapter 7), which in turn was based on the various local registration schemes that existed prior to the start of the Second World War (see Chapter 5). The national organization of dock labour, brought in under the Emergency Powers (Defence) Act during the War, made it difficult for ports to return to the complex and varied local schemes of the pre-war era. In June 1947 the Dock Workers (Regulation of Employment) Act created the NDLS. The Act's preamble stated that the purpose of the scheme was 'to create greater regularity of employment, and an adequate supply of labour to facilitate the rapid turn-round of ships, and the speedy transit of goods through the ports'.

THE NATIONAL AND LOCAL DOCK LABOUR BOARDS
The overall charge of the scheme was in the hands of the London-based National Dock Labour Board (NDLB), which comprised a chairman, vice-chairman and eight to ten members made up equally of labour representatives from the TGWU (see Chapter 5) and representatives of the employers of dock labour. The board's main duties were to:

• Control the number of registered dock workers and employers in ports, based on demand.
• Move dock labour between ports as demand required.
• Organize training.
• Organize welfare.
• Ensure that amenities were provided.

Each port or group of ports had its own local dock labour board that was a scaled-down version of the National Board. The local boards were also made up of a chairman and equal numbers of representatives from the labour and employers' sides. The principal task of the local boards was to organize registered dock workers and registered employers at port level and generally carry out the wishes of the national board. The organization of the local boards altered slightly during the scheme's existence, but the general arrangement was as follows:

Local Boards in 1952	Ports Covered
Tyne & Wear	Blyth, North Shields, Newcastle upon Tyne, Dunston, Gateshead, South Shields, Sunderland and Seaham.

Middlesbrough & Hartlepools	Middlesbrough and the Hartlepools.
Hull & Goole	Hull and Goole.
Immingham & Grimsby	Immingham and Grimsby.
Wash Ports	Boston, Sutton Bridge, Wisbech and Kings Lynn.
East Anglia	Great Yarmouth, Lowestoft and Ipswich.
London	Surrey, Upper Pool, Tilbury, Royal, India and Millwall, London & St. Katherine and Lighterage.
Medway & Swale	Rochester, Chatham, Strood, Queensborough, Sittingbourne and Whitstable.
South Coast	Southamptom, Poole & Hamworthy and Weymouth.
Plymouth	Plymouth.
Cornwall	Fowey, Par, Charlestown, Porthleven, Penzance, Newlyn, Mousehole, Truro, Penryn, Falmouth, Hayle, St. Ives and Portreath.
Bristol & Severn	Bristol, Sharpness and Gloucester.
South Wales	Newport, Cardiff & Penarth, Barry, Port Talbot and Swansea.
Liverpool, Garston & Widnes	Birkenhead, Bromborough, Liverpool, Garston and Widnes. Manchester Ellesmere Port, Weston Point, Runcorn, Partington and Salford.
Fleetwood	Fleetwood.
Preston	Preston.
Cumberland	Whitehaven, Workington,

	Maryport and Silloth.
Barrow-In-Furness	Barrow-In-Furness.
Ayrshire	Ayr, Troon, Irvine and Ardrossan.
Greenock	Greenock.
Glasgow	Glasgow.
Aberdeen	Aberdeen.
East Scotland	Dundee, Tayport, Methyl, Kirkcaldy, Burntisland, Grangemouth, Bo'ness, Granton and Leith.

THE HIRING SYSTEM

The local boards also oversaw the hiring of registered causal dock workers by registered employers. When the scheme was created, newly-built hiring halls known as 'controls' were erected across the docklands of each port. There, dockers requiring work were expected to attend one of the twice-daily calls (morning and midday) to be hired by the registered employers' foreman, who would take the Labour Board books or brass tallies of the dockers who were required for a job. Those dockers not chosen for work could be relocated to another control or even another port to be given a job. Should no work be available, the local boards would issue a stamp to the docker's book which ensured that a docker would be paid a reduced rate of fall-back pay and be expected to make themselves available for work at the next call. The stamp had different nicknames at each port. For instance, in London it was a 'bomp', at Hull a 'dint' and at Leith it was known as a 'duck egg' due to its colour. Consequently, those without work were said to be 'bomping' or 'dinting'.

The principles of the hiring system under the scheme was not radically different to those of the pre-Second World War era, excepting the presence of the hiring halls. Consequently, many of the old grievances between dockers endured and in some cases were made worse (see Chapter 3). Many casual dockers, who were made to fight and climb over each other for work in the controls, continued to resent the permanently-employed men who were not required to do so. Indeed, the scramble for work in the controls led to them being nicknamed 'the pen' by the dockers who felt like they were being herded like cattle or beasts in a pen. Accusations of favouritism worsened as the controls concentrated the hiring process and allowed dockers to see exactly which men known as 'blue-eyes' were given the better-paying jobs. In contrast, employers and the 'blue eyes' themselves maintained that the best workers earned the best jobs.

Oh it was horrendous – it really was – you used to go in you got there early in a morning – you had your [National Dock Labour Board] book and the foreman used to come out and he'd pick all his pals first and you'd maybe be a good worker and sometimes you got a job if he remembered you and other times you didn't and another time if there was a lot of work – you all went to work but you got some of the rubbish jobs and all the jobs were picked over. So there was a lot of dissatisfaction at that time.

Yeah it was the pen, what they called 'the pen'. It was like a cattle pen. There was a wall and behind that wall was a stand and the Foreman used to come up out the office and onto the stand so they were above you. Way down below in the hall were the dockers fighting for bloody jobs and you'd all have your dockers' book in your hand and the foreman comes up. If it's a good job everyone one puts their hand up with a book and he picks who he wants, such as that, and takes the books.

The pen – it was a big room and a raised thing at the end and the foreman was on that raised platform and he'd say 'I want 20 men for this' and we all knew from that foreman which was the best job – a fruit ship – more money or wool ship and you all went rushing forward and you was all literally climbing over each other to get that foreman to take your book – it was degrading and after about nearly a year I couldn't stand it.

DISCIPLINE

Many employers of dock labour resented the unions' joint control of the scheme. A particular grievance was the lack of an effective disciplinary mechanism under the scheme to stamp out pilfering and protective practices such as the welt and spelling (see Chapter 3). Fair punishment was difficult to implement within the casual system. For example, if a man was blacklisted for an offence by one employer, he could simply find work with another. If a man was dismissed, however, he paid for his transgression against one employer by forfeiting his right to work for any employer in the industry. Prior to the scheme's introduction the threat of not being hired at the call had generally ensured good industrial behaviour. However, the scheme's guarantee of fallback pay or reallocation to another dock made non-selection less serious. Furthermore, under the scheme, all decisions regarding discipline could be referred to the local labour boards for adjudication.

One former employer of dock labour recalled the ineffective disciplinary system under the scheme:

> The thing that got me was that there was no effective disciplinary system because although I might employ you as a Registered Dock Worker – if I'd thought you'd done something bad enough I could give you a warning or a two day suspension or something that couldn't be enforced until … well the man automatically appealed to the Local Dock Labour Board against it – automatically. So whatever the employer decided you could go through the motions

but that would go back to the local Dock Labour Board office for a disciplinary committee which surprise, surprise! Was like everything else 50/50 so five dockers sat that side of the table, five employers sat this side. How are you going to get anything passed. They would never split ranks and we would never split ranks so to do anything positive you've got to have a majority haven't you. So they just wouldn't uphold any disciplinary proceedings at all.

Another former employer of dock labour recollected:

If anybody was disciplined they went back to the National Dock Labour Board. We couldn't sack a man – he was our employee all we could do is send him back to the National Dock Labour Board. The real problem was that the Chairmen did not have a casting vote – so they could never agree anything to get a man sacked. The dockers would have to sack their own man – so a man could go to prison for theft – I know one guy who went to prison for 6 months, came out, went to the National Dock Labour Board to be sacked – 'Oh no, it's his first offence – he needs another go'. But he was reinstated and sent back by the National Dock Labour Board – basically because a docker would have to sack a docker and they wouldn't do it!

TRAINING
The official training and education of dock workers was also initiated under the scheme, with instruction on cargo handling and equipment offered. Many new purpose-built training schools with permanent staff were opened and London, Liverpool, Hull, Southampton, Bristol, Manchester and Grangemouth all had schools by the mid-1960s. The schools at the larger ports served other ports in the vicinity and dockers could travel on day release to attend courses.

WELFARE

In a bid to deal with the many accidents and injuries involving dock workers the NDLB gradually implemented medical measures on the docks. The board set up new medical centres staffed by state-registered nurses at each of the ports after 1947. In addition, first-aid boxes were also positioned around many dock estates and a number of dockers trained as first aiders. Measures were, however, negligible by the middle of the 1960s, particularly when considering the size of the dock labour forces at many ports and the seriousness and regularity of accidents on the docks.

A former docks nurse explains:

> We just had a great big bag and I used to go around on a little scooter, no helmets or anything like that. What we used to do, we dealt with bandaging and all that sort of thing you know whatever they came in. I had a thousand in one month – just me! You see we didn't have all the paramedics and things like that, that was our job really you-know. It was shocking, they used to come in say 'sister can we have one of your magic lotions' so I said 'yes alright just leave me for 10 minutes' and I boiled the kettle up and made tea, with no milk or sugar or anything and I cooled it down in a big Winchester bottle and I used to take it back and they didn't know and they couldn't realise that it was just tea but it's wonderful for your eyes, just packs on them just the little tea. We didn't have much [equipment] except that in the days before Morphia came in. When I first went on we didn't have any [medical] place, I just used to have to run, with me big pack on me back. We did get some injuries – terrible ones – we used to go down the holds and everything and we dealt with people, I had to go with them and deal with them. We had two barges, three ships abreast and two barges and the accident was in the . . .

[Motions climbing across several vessels] and climb into the barge and there were two people injured so we got the first one out and we were on a piece of wood as big as that twice . . . and just the chains and this little man had crushed his ribs and so I got behind him and had him like this [holding up torso] cos he didn't want to lay down obviously so we were in the middle and the crane brought us out . . . and this little voice at the front said to me 'Sister, I'm bloody frightened to death' and I said 'you're perfectly alright don't worry'.

AMENITIES

In 1947 the welfare of dock workers became the responsibility of the NDLB. During 1948 and 1949 the Board conducted a survey on amenities across the ports to provide a general view of the nature and amount of amenities available to dock workers. The survey indicated that conditions in most ports were atrocious. Even so, progress in providing dockers with basic facilities was slow and there still remained an almost complete absence of proper amenities across the ports during the early 1960s. A far reaching government inquiry into dock labour during the middle of the 1960s highlighted the appalling conditions and lack of amenities across the ports.

SPORTS AND SOCIAL CLUBS

The NDLB also took steps to look after the dockers' welfare outside of work. This was chiefly done by providing funds for the dockers to establish sports and social clubs in the ports. The clubs were run by committees of dockers who employed a steward. The steward would manage the club's staff and building, which offered bars, function rooms and entertainment. The clubs also hosted a wide number of dockers' sporting teams including bowls, cricket, snooker, darts, football, golf, rugby, judo, rowing and swimming, as well as recreational sections such as horticulture, lifesaving and first aid. The clubs became a hive of activity for the dockers and a real focal point for their community (see Chapter 6). The dockers' families would also attend the clubs and take part in the activities.

The wife and daughter of dockers describes:

I met a lot of dockworkers families cos my Dad he started all that off and he used to sign all the big stars like David Whitfield and Norman Collier, at that time kids couldn't go into the concert hall but I used to listen to David Whitfield cos they left the window open and I was outside we were allowed to go upstairs in the snooker room and things like that. Yeah, that's where I met [husband] George ... In the archery club! [Laughs] George had the rowing and the rugby. It was great for the sports and the social life of the Dockers.

The daughter of a docker remembered:

I remember it being quite a big part of our life. We used to go there as kids a lot. I can remember Dad was often in the bar and Mum were in the bar doing whatever inside and we'd be round the back pond fishing or playing. There was a big lake at the back and we used to go tiddling – tiddly fishing with a pin, a matchstick and a worm and come back with a jar full of tiddlers... or ... I can remember going up into the sports room.

THE RECORDS
NDLB Archives
The records of the NDLB and the National Dock Labour Corporation which preceded it can be found at the National Archives at Kew. The National Archives also hold the records of the

A photograph of a dockers' rugby team, 1965. Many dockers were involved in the sports teams hosted by the Dock Labour Scheme's sports and social clubs.

An NDLB rowing team: rowing was a popular sport amongst the dockers.

local boards of London, Cumbria, Grimsby & Immingham, and the South Coast (Southampton, Poole & Hamworthy, Weymouth). The records of most other local boards can be found at city and county archives in the vicinity of each local board, the relevant archive reference in (). The majority of archives hold local area board minutes which provide details of the day-to-day business of the local boards. Much of this information is very general, but the names of individual dockers appear in items relating to the registration and discipline. Many of these archives also hold other records relating to dockers, so make use of services who offer an online catalogue. Researchers must be aware that some records contain personal or sensitive information and may be closed to the public under Data Protection legislation. In some cases a Freedom of Information requests can be made to view content in closed documents.

The National Archives

Kew, Richmond, Surrey TW9 4DU
Tel: 020 8876 3444
Web: www.nationalarchives.gov.uk
The National Archives at Kew hold by far the largest collect of records relating to the administration of the Dock Labour Scheme at a national and local level under BK. Online catalogue: http://discovery.nationalarchives.gov.uk/

The Records of the National Dock Labour Corporation, 1941– 1947 (BK1): Amongst these records can be found documents relating to discipline, welfare, pay and conditions of employment of dock workers. There are also sections that provide information on other port transport workers organized under the Corporation including coal trimmers, cargo superintendants, fish lumpers and porters, railway workers and riggers.

The Records of the National Dock Labour Board, 1947–1989 (BK2–BK37): The records of the NDLB are extensive and relate to the organization and administration of the scheme at a national level. However, sections of note for family historians include documents regarding discipline, port medical services, welfare, dock labour board staff and training (BK2); *Training of Dock Workers*, Great Britain (1966) publication (BK4/7); Photograph Collection, 1953–1963 (BK12/14); Surveys and Reports of Dock Amenities (BK16); New Premises Documents Folder (including plans of new buildings such as call stands, medical centres and social clubs at various ports) (BK17); Training and Welfare Department records and programmes (BK23).

London Dock Labour Board, 1939–1947: Records of the London Dock Labour Board relating to the regulation of labour within the Port of London. Useful Documents include a small selection of record cards and dossiers of individual London dock workers (BK35); material concerning disciplinary cases which have come before an appeal tribunal (BK21 and BK22); Records of the London Port Workers' Sports Federation (BK18)

Cumbria Dock Labour Board, 1942–1989: Records of the Cumbria Dock Labour Board regarding the administration of dock work in the ports of Barrow-in-Furness, Workington, Whitehaven, Maryport and Silloth. Notable sections include Discipline and Appeals, 1968–1976 (BK9/7); Accidents and Lost Time at Workington, 1958–1959 (BK9/11); Accidents and Lost Time at Whitehaven, 1953–1961 (BK9/12); Welfare, 1946–1988 (BK9/16); Barrow Dock Sports and Social Club (including photographs) 1955–1975 (BK9/17); Dock Amenities, 1948–1984 (BK9/21–BK9/24). See also Cumbria Archive and Local Studies Centre below.

Grimsby & Immingham Dock Labour Board, 1942–1989: The records cover the local dock labour scheme at the port of Grimsby and Immingham. Although the early sections of these collections are dominated by general operational documents the latter are of limited use to genealogists, they also contain numerous documents that provide an insight into welfare and recreational activities of dock workers at the two ports: Dock Amenities, 1961–1968 (BK10/17–18); Sports, 1967–1975 (BK10/19); Sea Angling Competition, 1983–1989 (BK10/20-21); Football Competitions, 1972–1987 (BK10/22–24); Social, Sport and Recreation Association; Port Medical Services, 1988–1989 (BK10/29); Port Medical Services, 1973–1979 (BK10/30).

South Coast Dock Labour Board, 1940–1989: Archives covering the ports of Southampton, Poole & Hamworthy, and Weymouth with interesting section on Meritorious Service awards, 1957–1977 (BK11/2) and Claims by Dock Workers, 1958–1970 (BK11/12).

Hull
Hull History Centre
Worship St, Hull, HU2 8BG
Tel: 01482 317500
Email: hullhistorycentre@hcandl.co.uk
Web: www.hullhistorycentre.org.uk
The principal archives of the Hull and Goole Dock Labour Board, the largest collection outside of the National Archives (C DPN). Includes lists of registered dockers for the 1960s and 1970s (C DPN/17), card index of registered dockers 1940s to 1960s (C DPN/18) and card index of employers 1942–1960 (C DPN/16). Also, tribunal cases (C DPN/13/9–11). There are some very detailed reports on dock amenities from 1966 that show the harsh conditions in the port (C DPN/11). A small number of photographs can be found under C DPN/15 and a series of

publications relating to dock labour in C DPN/19. The Centre's Transport and General Workers' Union archive also contains documents of the Hull and Goole Dock Labour Board dated 1959–1989 (U DTG/7). These are mainly minutes relating to the board's various activities. Online catalogue: http://catalogue. hullhistorycentre.org.uk/.

The East Riding
East Riding Archives and Local Studies
County Hall, Beverley, East Riding of Yorkshire, HU17 9BA
Tel: 01482 392790
Email: archives.service@eastriding.gov.uk
Web: www2.eastriding.gov.uk/leisure/archives-family-and-local-history/
The East Riding Archives and Local Studies service holds other records relating to the Hull and Goole Dock Labour Board, 1943 East Riding Archives and Local Studies 1989 (ND). These include minute books 1943–1989, Goole registration committee minute book 1947, East Riding Archives and Local Studies 1949, registration committee minute book 1951, East Riding Archives and Local Studies 1955, Hull registration committee minute books 1955, East Riding Archives and Local Studies 1986, training committee minute book 1975, East Riding Archives and Local Studies 1982, indexes to minutes 1969 and East Riding Archives and Local Studies 1989. Online catalogue: www.eastriding.gov.uk/CalmView/.

Tyne & Wear
Discovery Museum,
Blandford Square, Newcastle Upon Tyne, NE1 4JA
Email: info@twarchives.org.uk
Tel: (0191) 277 2248
Web: https://twarchives.org.uk/
This archive contains National Dock Labour Corporation Ltd: Tyne, Wear, Blyth and Seaham Harbour Area Board minutes 1946

to 1947 (G.DLC0) and Tyne & Wear Dock Board: minutes 1947, 1989 (G.DLB), which cover Blyth, North Shields, Newcastle upon Tyne, Dunston, Gateshead, South Shields, Sunderland and Seaham.

The Medway
Medway Archives Centre
32 Bryant Road, Strood, ME2 3EP
Email: malsc@medway.gov.uk
Tel: 01634 332 714
Web: www.medway.gov.uk/info/200182/arts_and_heritage/317/medway_archives_centre
Medway Archives Centre houses the Medway & Swale Dock Labour Board minutes, 1969–1989 (DLBM/1) covering the dockers at Rochester, Chatham, Strood, Queensborough, Sittingbourne and Whitstable.

Plymouth and West Devon
Plymouth and West Devon Record Office
Unit 3, Clare Place, Plymouth, PL4 0JW
Email: pwdro@plymouth.gov.uk
Tel: 01752 305940
Web: https://plymhearts.org/archives/
Plymouth Dock Labour Board minutes, 1951–1989 (1596) are held by Plymouth and West Devon Record Office, for further details see online catalogue: http://web.plymouth.gov.uk/archives catalogue.

Cornwall
Cornwall Records Office
Old County Hall, Truro, Cornwall, TR1 3AY
Email: cro@cornwall.gov.uk
Tel: 01872 323127
Web: www.cornwall.gov.uk/community-and-living/records-archives -and-cornish-studies/
Cornwall Records Office houses Cornwall Dock Labour Board

minutes, 1947–1989 covering Fowey, Par, Charlestown, Porthleven, Penzance, Newlyn, Mousehole, Truro, Penryn, Falmouth, Hayle, St. Ives and Portreath. For more details about this collection see the online catalogue:http://crocat.cornwall. gov.uk/DServe/dserve.exe?dsqApp=Archive&dsqDb=Catalog&d sqCmd=Search.tcl.

Bristol
Bristol Archives
'B' Bond Warehouse, Smeaton Road, Bristol, BS1 6XN
Email: archives@bristol.gov.uk
Tel: 0117 922 4224
Web: www.bristolmuseums.org.uk/bristol-archives/
The records of the Bristol & Severn Dock Labour Board and its predecessor organizations (40194) are held at Bristol archives. This collection includes Bristol's first local registration scheme (1916–1941), the Bristol Branch of the wartime Dock Labour Corporation (1941–1947), and Bristol Dock Labour Board (1947–1989). The archives' online catalogue provides further information: http://archives.bristol.gov.uk/default.aspx.

Merseyside
Maritime Archives and Library, Merseyside Maritime Museum
Albert Dock, Liverpool, L3 4AQ
Email: maritime.archives@liverpoolmuseums.org.uk
Tel: 0151 478 4424
Web: www.liverpoolmuseums.org.uk/maritime/archive/
The Maritime Archives and Library at Merseyside Maritime Museum house the local board minutes for the Liverpool, Garston and Widnes Dock Labour Board, 1948–1989 (P-NDLB).

Lancashire
Lancashire Archives
Bow Lane, Preston, Lancashire, PR1 2RE
Email: record.office@lancashire.gov.uk
Tel: 01772 533039
Web: www.lancashire.gov.uk/libraries-and-archives/archives-and
-record-office/
The Fleetwood and Preston Dock Labour Board records are split across several collections. The Fleetwood Dock Labour Board's minutes, 1963–1989 can be found under (DDX 1856/acc8118/box 4), whilst the Fleetwood Fishing Vessel Owner's Association also contains labour board records relating to Fleetwood dock labourers (DDX 1263/ACC4270/110). Labour board records regarding Wyre Dock are under (DDX 2491/862). Within the Port of Preston's records can be found documents relating the Preston Dock Labour Board (DDPP/9). Preston and Fleetwood board minutes and financial records, c.1940s–1989 are under (DL). Online catalogue: archivecat.lancashire.gov.uk/calmview/

Cumbria
Cumbria Archive and Local Studies Centre
Ramsden Square, Barrow-in-Furness, Cumbria, LA14 1LL
Email: barrow.archives@cumbria.gov.uk
Tel: 01229 407377
Web: www.cumbria.gov.uk/archives/archivecentres/balsc.asp
Aside from the collection held at the National Archives, Cumbria Archive and Local Studies Centre also hold records relating to the Barrow Local Board, 1942–1963; Cumberland and Barrow Dock Labour Board, 1960–1963; Cumberland Ports Dock Labour Board, 1960–1963 (BTNDLB). See online catalogue: www.archiveweb.cumbria.gov.uk/CalmView/default.aspx.

On Film
British Transport Films' docu-drama *Berth 24* (1950) provides a

unique display of the hiring process at one of the NDLB's controls. The film is available to view on the British Film Institute's website www.screenonline.org.uk or on the widely-available DVD '*Just the Ticket*': *British Transport Films Collection, Volume 9*. There is also a good visual example of the NDLB's activities outside of the workplace. The Yorkshire Film Archive holds a fascinating and rare piece of film relating to the sporting activities of the dockers under the National Dock Labour Scheme: the 1955 Newlands Cup Final match between teams of dockers from the ports of Goole and Swansea. The film features extensive highlights of the match and includes footage of the post-match dinner party and trophy award ceremony. Available to watch for free on the Yorkshire Film Archive's website: www.yorkshire filmarchive.com/film/newlands-cup-final.

Objects and Items

During its administration of the country's dock labour force the NDLB produced and distributed many objects. Of particular use to genealogists are the items relating to the Board's social clubs and their different sports and recreation sections. Dockers who took part in such activities were regularly photographed and awarded badges, trophies, plaques, certificates, programmes and plates. You may be fortunate to inherit some of these items; if not, it is often possible to view such items at the small number of dockers' social clubs that are still running. These include:

The Dockers Club (Belfast)

57 Pilot Street, Belfast, County Antrim, BT1 3AH
Tel: 028 9074285

Leith Dockers Club

17 Academy Street, Leith, Edinburgh, EH6 7EE
Tel: 0131 467 7879
Email: leithdockers@hotmail.com
Web: www.leithdockersclub.co.uk

Sharpness Dockers Club
Berkeley, Gloucestershire, GL13 9UN
Tel: 01453 811477
Email: sharpnessdockersclub@gmail.co.uk
Web: www.thesharpnessdockersclub.co.uk

Swansea Dockers Club
Delhi Street, St. Thomas, Swansea, SA1 8BT
Tel: 01792 641462 or 01792 655467
Web: www.swanseadockers.co.uk

The Willows Social Club (Hull)
695a Holderness Road, Hull, HU8 9AN
Tel: 01482 781019

The Dockers' Club at Leith, one of many around the country's ports.

Newspapers (see Chapter 1)
Local and regional newspapers reported widely on the sporting activities and results of the NDLB's sports sections, and articles frequently printed the line-ups of the teams. for access to newspapers.

RECOMMENDED READS
David Wilson's book *Dockers: The Impact of Industrial Change* (Fontana/Collins, 1972) offers the most detailed description of the Scheme's origins, functions and operation.

Chapter 9

DOCK STRIKES AND THE DECLINE OF THE DOCKERS – 1967–1989

During the early 1960s the organization and working practices of Britain's dock labour force still closely resembled those of the Victorian period, with the exception of some limited mechanization in cargo-handling and the presence of the National Dock Labour Scheme. Across the ports the majority of cargoes continued to be handled manually by gangs of dockworkers who were largely employed on a casual basis. However, the second half of the 1960s witnessed the implementation of large-scale government reforms that swept away, virtually overnight, traditions that had endured on the waterfront for generations. Of greater concern for the dock labour force, was that reform also opened the gates to technological forces that caused the decline and eventual disappearance of the dockers on the British waterfront.

CONTAINERS AND THE CARGO-HANDLING REVOLUTION

By the early 1960s the need for the reorganization of the country's dock labour force was seen as a top priority by the government. This was largely due to the revolutionary developments in cargo handling technology that had first emerged during the Second World War. The efficient transportation of vehicles and supplies across the English Channel had been essential to the achievement

The roll-on roll-off vessel MV Dana Maxima *at Grimsby.*

of Allied victory in Nazi-occupied Europe. In the build-up to D-Day on 6 June 1944 the United States had developed and implemented various new ways of moving goods between ship and shore. Most were based on the principle of unitisation: moving goods in single pre-packed metal boxes, fully-laden vehicles or on top of wooden pallets. These methods saved much time in transporting essential supplies from British bases to the Allied front as they did not need to be unpacked or repacked between the point of origin and the destination.

After the war ended moves were made in the United States to adapt wartime transport technology for commercial use. This was

A fork-lift truck on the docks c.1970s. This and other technology replaced tough manual labour.

A modern container park.

driven by a desire to reduce the time and cost of conventional cargo handling by American dock labourers, known as longshoremen. The lead was taken by American businessman and transport entrepreneur Frank Purcell McLean who in 1956 purchased and modified two oil tankers to carry goods in metal boxes or 'containers'. These could be loaded at a factory or depot, carried by truck to a port for transfer to a ship, which would then dock at a port of call where another truck would receive the box for carriage to its destination. In parallel, other ships designed to carry fully laden road vehicles that could 'roll-on and roll-off' the vessel were also developed in America. Both systems were refined and developed during the 1950s and 1960s with the construction of purpose-built vessels and the standardization of container sizes. Thus, the container age was born.

DEVLIN AND DECASUALISATION

The man tasked with adapting the dockers to the container age was a retired judge, the Right Honourable Lord Patrick Devlin. Following an extensive inquiry, Devlin's findings were published in *Committee of Inquiry under Lord Devlin into Certain Matters Concerning the Port Transport Industry*. Devlin identified that the successful operation of costly new cargo handling facilities like container terminals and roll-on/roll-off ('ro-ro)' berths, required a regular workforce with regular pay. Consequently, the two main recommendations of the report were, firstly to abolish the casual system or 'decasualise' the dockers by assigning them to a reduced number of permanent employers, and secondly to restructure wages systems at each port in line with mechanized cargo handling. Decasualisation or 'D-day' took place on 18 September 1967 and ended a system that had been in place for over a century. This was followed in 1970 by the reorganization of pay at port level. Following extensive negotiations between unions and employers some piece-rate ports like London and Hull switched to a fixed rate of pay while the Liverpool dockers switched from fixed pay to piece-work.

Devlin had also recognized that the efficient operation of new facilities needed industrial peace, something that had eluded the British waterfront for almost a century. Consequently, Devlin recommended that moves be made to restore the authority of the TGWU over its rank-and-file members, particularly at Liverpool and Hull where there was a fierce rivalry between the 'Whites' of the TGWU and the 'Blues' of the National Amalgamated Stevedores and Dockers Union (see Chapter 5). The TGWU sent Tom Cronin, one of its ablest London officers, to the ports to restore union authority. To a large extent this objective was achieved. Over the course of ten months Cronin reorganized the union's branches, established a system of shop stewards and sent a damning report to London headquarters that resulted in the sacking and replacement of the three full-time officials at Hull.

Alongside union reforms Devlin also recommended that a thorough survey of amenities in scheme ports should be undertaken by the National Dock Labour Board (see Chapter 8). The Board's survey was taken in 1966 and detailed the true nature of conditions to which dockers were subjected. In the years that followed the Board put plans into action and all scheme ports were provided with purpose-built dockside canteens and restaurants, which also offered other facilities such as lockers and showers. This development finally provided dockers with amenities comparable with other industries. However, modernization and reform did not bring about industrial peace on the waterfront. In fact, Devlin's scheme heralded a new era of heightened unrest across the port industry.

Devlin came along – a man who's never worked in his soddin' life, 'e came along and 'is idea was everybody would get the same wages – everybody would do the same work and they took the incentive away. But as I say – Devlin – that man destroyed the docks, that man had never worked in 'is life – no experience of working people. 'e just took the incentive away and eventually you got the lazy man and you got in a situation where you said 'I'm not gonna work 'ard here! Why should I work 'ard when that prat over there is sat on 'is arse?!' So it just disappeared then.'

[Devlin] gave me stable money whereas before when you was ordinary under the National Dock Labour Board, you dint know what money you was getting but at least [after Devlin] I knew I was getting – a certain amount every week without any overtime. So you could work out what you could afford and luckily we were able to afford this [house].

All this [change] happened . . . what I'm telling you now, all this happened in my 8/9 years on the dock from 1964 to 1970, *everything* happened! That was the period of thousands of men . . . years unloading ships . . . [when] cargo went to a ship and it was loaded [manually] and then it was unloaded [manually] it *stopped*. A miracle invention came along called the container. All the dockers' jobs went overnight. Summat that'd gone on for hundreds of years, thousands of years it stopped in my ten years on the dock. The whole world stopped in ten years . . . I can't believe it.

NATIONAL DOCK STRIKES AND MILITANCY

D-day was met with strikes in London, Liverpool and Hull, where many dockers cherished the freedom of the casual system which allowed them to pick and choose their work. This was followed by a serious dispute between the TGWU and employers over the national weekly time rate of pay. This led to a three-week national dock strike by 47,000 dockers beginning on 15 July 1970, the first since 1926. This ended two weeks later when the dockers eventually accepted a pay deal offered by a court of enquiry. As the dockers involved in the national strike returned to work, it was hoped that peace would prevail across dockland. This was not to be as new threats to the dockers' jobs emerged.

The introduction of new mechanized and unitised cargo-handling methods accelerated hugely after 1970. As machine replaced muscle, the requirement for large numbers of workers on the docks was rapidly reduced. Furthermore, unemployment was increased as registered dockers lost work to unregistered labourers outside of the ports. The development of mechanized cargo-handling had encouraged many small wharves on rivers and estuaries, which had been considered too small to be included in the National Dock Labour Scheme in 1947 (see Chapter 8), to invest in the new equipment to load and discharge vessels. In addition, containers also began to be loaded and unloaded or 'stuffed and unstuffed' at newly-established inland depots. As those employed at such sites were not deemed to be involved in dock work as defined by the National Dock Labour Scheme, many non-registered labourers, who could be employed on a cheaper basis, found work. Incensed that their work was being poached by outsiders, the dockers fought a militant campaign throughout the 1970s and 1980s to protect their jobs.

Based on these developments, labour relations within the industry deteriorated rapidly and another national dock strike took place in July 1972. The stoppage lasted three weeks and involved the country's 42,000 dock workers. Industrial action was widespread across the ports leading up to, and during, the strike. The London, Liverpool and Hull dockers picketed sites using unregistered labour and 'blacked' any shipping or haulage companies that used such workers. Such tactics led to some dramatic and well-publicized incidents that are now part of dockland lore. In London five shop stewards, Conny Clancy, Tony Merrick, Bernie Steer, Vic Turner and Derek Watkins, were sent to Pentonville Prison by the National Industrial Relations Court after they refused to obey a court order to cease picketing Midland

Cold Storage Company in East London. Widespread protests by thousands of striking workers followed the imprisonment of the 'Pentonville Five', who were released a week later. In the North dockers too fell afoul of the law. Having begun an intensive picketing campaign of the unregistered ports and wharves around the Humber, Hull and Goole dockers spent a large part of the actual strike mass-protesting against the use of unregistered labour at the Trent wharves of Neap House and Gunness. This action descended into three days of running battles at the two sites between police, road haulage drivers and the dockers. The events of the tumultuous events on Humberside were recorded in great detail by Hull docker Terry Turner in his valuable record *Diary of the Docks' Dispute, 1972–1973*:

> At 1.30pm with the pickets growing more restless and frustrated because the wharf was working normally events started to warm up. At a signal from one of them several shop stewards and other dockers charged up the wharf's bank where the Police were more thinly lined in an attempt to get on to the wharf. When the men made their rush the drivers who had sat on the bank smirking hurriedly retreated and the Police thwarted the pickets' attack by using any method they could. They pushed and punched the dockers back down the bank, there were really vicious blows struck by both sides. Police and dockers wrestled on the floor; some dockers were bundled roughly into police vans. One long-haired picket was dragged cruelly by his mane up the steep bank by a burly policeman before being taken away. An elderly docker was half-throttled into unconsciousness by another policeman and he sat in the roadside before he was taken to Scunthorpe hospital. By this time other pickets had gone to the aid of their colleagues and several running fights took place. The whole of men's bodies – fists, feet, knees, heads and fingers

became weapons to try and overcome one another. Police arrested several more dockers by simply overpowering them with numbers and the dockers were taken into custody. The Police had retained their wall and repulsed the dockers' attempts to enter the wharf.

Ports are hit after dockers' arrest

The refusal of five shop stewards to obey a National Industrial Relations Court order to cease picketing Midland Cold Storage Company in East London led to their arrest and jailing at Pentonville Prison.
The Birmingham Post, *22 July 1972*

Another nationwide stoppage was threatened and only narrowly averted in 1980, but a national dock strike ensued in July 1984 in response to British Steel's use of unregistered labour to unload iron ore at Immingham. A further national strike followed in August of the same year following the use of unregistered labour to discharge a shipment of coal from a 'blacked' vessel at Hunterston in Scotland. By this time, however, the country's dock labour force had been greatly reduced, with many dockers having taken voluntary redundancy.

WORKING LIFE ON THE MODERNIZED DOCKS
Amidst the strikes and militancy of the 1970s and 1980s many dockers became increasingly despondent with dock work as the labour force and docks were transformed. Modernization had caused the disappearance of the work territories that the dockers had held for generations. New large container and roll-on/roll-off vessels, which needed deep-water facilities and land space for vehicle access and unit storage, caused the relocation of dock work to terminals and berths at new sites on the edge of the old port towns and cities, or to new container ports like Felixstowe and Tilbury. At the older ports, town docks that were built when ships were much smaller, fell into disuse and became silted up, their quays and warehouses falling into dereliction.

At these new sites the daily work of the ever-decreasing dock labour force was transformed, becoming more routine and less

Modern dock workers wearing hi-vis jackets working on containers c.1990.

varied. Tough physical labour in gangs was replaced by solitary work in the cabins of forklift trucks, cranes, diggers or the 'mafis', tugs and straddle carriers that were used to carry trailers and containers across the docks. The varied array of goods that once lined the quays, wharves and warehouses of many ports were now hidden inside metal boxes or by the curtains of flatbed lorry trailers. However, mechanical handling and the introduction of the Health and Safety at Work Act in 1974 did make the docks a safer place to work. Once famous for their flat caps, overcoats and scarves, the dockers were soon clad in hard hats, high-visibility jackets, gloves and steel-toecapped boots. The dockers' leisure time on the docks was also different. The large, new purpose-built restaurants introduced by the National Dock Labour Board lacked the hustle and bustle of the old dockside cafes and coffee shops.

'Mafis' at work on the docks.

The arrival of new cargo-handling and transport technology from the 1960s rendered many old port facilities redundant and large areas of dockland fell into dereliction.

Me elder brother 'e was on the containers – a really, really easy job. You just made sure everything was going smooth you know what I mean? You dint do any physical work cos 'e was used to physical – real 'ard physical work and 'e wasn't keen on it and I said 'don't you think its time Bill? The docks have gone – its changed. Don't you think it's time you packed it in?' And 'e did. And then me brother-in-law did, me mate Hutchy did, me mates – all me mates they give it up. You dint 'ave so many men [after modernization]. Say you 'ad six men in a gang you 'ad 'undred men on a ship [before modernization] you was all talking to each other – coffee shops, muggers, pubs! Whereas it went down to maybe two or three men it just . . . it just seemed to stop.

THE END OF AN ERA: THE ABOLITION OF THE NATIONAL DOCK LABOUR SCHEME

Having seen how prosperous non-scheme wharves and ports like Felixstowe had been following the introduction of mechanical handling in the 1960s, the British government increasingly saw the National Dock Labour Scheme as a barrier between employers and the strike-prone dock labour force (see Chapter 8). Just as the Scheme had been introduced by the passing of an Act in 1947, so it was removed. Margaret Thatcher's Conservative government passed the Dock Work Act 1989 on 3 July 1989 and the Scheme was abolished. When announced, large numbers of disillusioned registered dock workers accepted generous redundancy payments and left the industry. Other dockers were issued with redundancy notices just hours after the announcement and in the following days more men accepted payments. Perhaps not surprisingly, these developments were met with a national strike across the ports and on midnight on 10 July the waterfronts of London, Liverpool, Southampton, Grimsby and Hull all fell silent. Although lasting three weeks until 1 August, the strike was

The bronze dockers' statue at the regenerated Royal Victoria Dock, London. The three figures depicted are local men with links to the docker community: John Ringwood, Mark Tibbs and Patrick Holland. The statue was unveiled in 2009 and is one of only a few monuments dedicated to dock labourers.

ineffectual as, by this time, thousands more dockers had either left the industry or returned to work under new contracts.

By the time of the Scheme's abolition many of the old abandoned port areas had been purchased by local governments and private investors and regenerated as places of leisure, business and accommodation. At the former general-cargo giants Liverpool and London, development corporations were set up to oversee major dockland redevelopment projects. Planning for Liverpool's Albert Dock's regeneration began in 1982 and it was officially re-opened on 24 May 1988 as a multi-functional complex that continues to house an art gallery, museums, television studios, hotels, shops and restaurants. On the vast area of derelict docks in London the Docklands Light Railway was built and Canary Wharf born whilst London City Airport opened in 1987 on the site of the Royal Docks. In 2009, a figurative bronze statue depicting three dockworkers was unveiled and dedicated to the communities of the Royal Docks and the men and women who worked there. Sadly, this is one of only a few tributes on the country's redeveloped docklands to the thousands of dockers who once toiled on them.

> We couldn't see it [abolition] comin'. I couldn't believe it 'ad come cos I'd just been to a meeting in Liverpool and 'e was an MP – Labour 'e was a New Zealander 'e was from New Zealand but 'e was a Labour MP in the Labour Government 'ere and 'e said 'look' and 'e said 'I can assure you that nobody can do anything to the National Dock Labour Board – it *cannot* be touched'. So, 'e said 'you've no need to worry about anything there'. Six weeks later Maggie Thatcher closed it – no consultation nothing! I don't know 'ow she did it she just did it and that was it – just gone. That's when most of the people left when it'd gone they left that was the finish, yeah.

THE RECORDS
Newspapers (see Chapter 1): The regular, widespread and large-scale industrial action of the dockers during these years meant that they not only featured in the newspapers of the day, but were more often than not on the front page. Indeed, dockers made the headlines more than another working group during the period, perhaps with the exception of the miners. Consequently, newspapers are without doubt the best source of information for those hoping to find out more about their docker ancestors during the twilight years of the old docks. Newspapers often featured photographs and interviews of striking dockers and their leaders.

On Film: There are two very interesting and informative films that cover the events discussed in this chapter. *The Dockers* (Praxis Films 1988) was released by Channel 4 on the eve of the abolition of the Scheme. It chronicles the story of the port of Hull, its docks and its dockers through archive footage and contemporary interviews. However, the film mainly concentrates on the period after the Second World War through the experiences of trade union activists involved in the campaigns that ended the casual system. *Arise Ye Workers* (Working Class Films/Cinema Action 1973) by the radical group film Cinema Action charts the events of the National Dock Strike of 1972 including the arrest of the 'Pentonville Five'. It is available to watch on the British Film Institute's website: www.screenonline.org.uk/film/id/711919/index.html.

RECOMMENDED READS

Death of the Docks (AuthourHouse, 2010) by Colin Ross is the first-hand account of a London docker's experience of the monumental changes that occurred on the docks during these years. Some dockers kept diaries during the national dock strikes that record the drama as it unfolded. One of the most detailed accounts of the strike and the wider events surrounding it is *Diary of the Docks' Dispute 1972-1973* (Hull University, 1980) by Terry Turner. For those desirous of learning more about the technology that transformed the working lives of their docker ancestors, Brian J. Cudahy's *Box Boats: How Container Ships Changed the World* (Fordham University Press, 2006) is the best publication on the subject. John Dempster's book, *The Rise and Fall of the Dock Labour Scheme* (Biteback, 2010) explains the pitfalls of the National Dock Labour Scheme and the political events that lead to its abolition.

Glossary

TYPES OF DOCK LABOURER

A dock labourer or 'docker' was the general term for anyone engaged on the various kinds of unskilled work on a dock such as carrying or wheeling goods from or to ships or assisting a high-skilled category of dock worker known as a stevedore in loading and unloading of vessels. However, there were dozens of subcategories of dock labourer who were often identified, and

A runnerman directing a crane on the docks. Runnermen were just one type of dock labourer amongst dozens.

named in relation to the types of goods handled, their place of work, or the specific skill(s) they performed in the cargo-handling process. In reality, job specialization was of bewildering complexity and probably only truly understood by those who worked on the docks. The following list, which has been drawn and adapted from the classifications of 'Water Transport Workers' used for the 1921 census, provides some coherence on the many types of dock labourer that emerged in line with the growing seaborne trades from the middle of the nineteenth century. As traditional manual cargo-handling methods generally altered very little before the introduction of mechanized means, many of the following job roles continued into the 1960s.

Bank rider, brakesman (coal drops): *see* **wagonman.**

Barge emptier, boat emptier: a **carrier** engaged in unloading barges, boats or other small vessels.

Bobber, fish bobber: an East Coast term, which originated when fish porters were paid 1s. per hour. *See* **lumper, fish.**

Boxman; cradleman: a dock labourer who stood on the dock quay or in the ship's hold, filling a box or similar receptacle with a number of small separate packages. They also attached slings to boxes, which were then hitched on to a crane fall for removal to hold or quay by a **hatchman** or by a **winchman.**

Bunker: a dock labourer who tipped coal from baskets or trucks into coal bins or bunkers as they were lowered by hoist. They also directed coal chutes into bunkers, *see* **trapper.**

Busheller, grain busheller: a **filler** in a dock shed who filled sacks with grain, discharged in bulk from ship using an iron measure known as a bushel (drum or flat), in readiness for weighing.

Cargo worker, general cargo worker: a general worker (as distinct from a specialist e.g. **fish loader** or **grain hopperman**) assisting in the loading or unloading of any cargoes.

Carrier; runner, runnerman: a **porter** who carried goods on their back, shoulder or head between quay, ship or warehouse, or about dock premises generally. Carriers were usually specifically designated according to the goods they carried (e.g. bag carrier, deal carrier, fish box carrier, fruit carrier).

Coal teemer: *see* **teemer**.

Coal tipper: *see* **tipper**.

Coal trimmer: *see* **trimmer**.

Collier: a general term for one of a coal barge crew, who assisted in unloading coal from barge to ship or to quay. Included **bunker**, **trimmer** and **loader**.

Cradleman: *see* **boxman**.

Deal gangwayman: stood on a gangway between ship and wharf or quay and passed timber from a dock labourer on the ship's deck to a deal **carrier**.

Discharger, coal boat: a general term for any labourer engaged in discharging coal, including **unloader** and **whipper**; usually used a crane fitted with a skip.

Dog lad: attached slings or dogs to coal baskets or trucks to enable them to be hoisted in or out of a ship's bunkers.

Donkeyman: in charge of a small auxiliary engine ('donkey' engine) used, mainly when a ship was in port, for working winches, pumps and other appliances on board ship.

Filler: a dock labourer engaged in any filling operations e.g. grain, in bulk into baskets or other receptacles in a ship's hold or on quay in readiness for trucking away by dock labourers or for attaching to crane slings and subsequent tipping (*see* tipper). Includes grain busheller.

Fish dockman, fish loader, fish quayman: Loaded fish boxes on lorries or other vehicles at fish wharves. *See also* **carrier.**

Grain hopperman: adjusted position of hopper to emptying buckets of elevator, and moved hopper along rails during process of filling grain from ship into warehouse.

Grain trimmer: *see* **trimmer.**

Hatchman, hatchminder, hatchwayman: Stood by hatch when ship is loading or unloading and signalled to **winchman** or **railman** when to set the winch in motion to raise or lower goods from or into hold. A hatchman would signal with his hand to a **holdsman** when goods were about to be raised or lowered.

Hobbler (slang): *see* **labourer.** Sometimes specifically designated e.g. fish hobbler, coal hobbler.

Hoist worker, coal (staithes); coal derrick labourer: Filled containers with coal by shovelling, and attached them to chain of hoist ready for slinging into a ship's hold.

Holdsman: a dock labourer working in a ship's hold, carrying or wheeling goods to hatchway or from hatchway to stevedore and stowing them under his direction. Holdsmen also attached and detached slings, dogs and hooks of hoists to receive goods, lowered into hold by **winchmen**.

Labourer, coal wharf (staithes): worked on a wharf where coal was discharged or loaded into ships either by hoist or tip. Coal wharf labourers also performed general duties like sweeping the wharf and supplying coke to cranes and hoists.

Labourer on coal lighter, dock: Filled, by shovelling, baskets or metal containers with coal prior to their being lifted by crane from lighter to ship, or trimmed coal in lighter to enable grabs to pick it up. *See* **trimmer**.

Lighter discharger: a dock labourer who unloaded goods from a lighter to a ship in a harbour or fairway.

Loader: general term for any person engaged in stowing cargo on any navigable craft (large, small, sea-going or otherwise); took care to stow cargo in smallest possible space, securely (to prevent shifting during voyage), uniformly (to avoid the vessel listing), and conveniently (so that cargo could be got out quickly, especially if vessel was to call at several places in succession); term chiefly indicated man loading barge, canal boat, or other small craft engaged in inland navigation, coasting or 'short sea' trades; sometimes specifically designated according to type of boat loaded, or place of loading, e.g. boat loader, canal boat loader, dockside loader, slate loader (quay); highest degree of skill was required in stowing cargo on large sea-going vessels carrying mixed cargo and visiting many ports; such work was generally done by **stevedores**.

Loader, coal; coal lumper: one of a team of men engaged in coaling a vessel by carrying it in baskets or other receptacles along gangway to ship and discharging it into holds or bunkers.

Lumper: similar to a **carrier** and was generally employed casually by a master stevedore.

Lumper, fish; bobber, fish bobber (East Coast), fish hobbler, runner: discharged fish from trawlers and drifters to the quay, often carried fish in 'kits' or baskets.

Pitwood roller-off: rolled logs of pitwood, from ship to wharf, down an inclined plane.

Porter: a dock labourer who was engaged in carrying or otherwise transporting goods at docks; sometimes specifically designated according to place where employed or to goods carried, e.g. canal porter, canal boat porter, corn porter, contract porter (paid per ton of goods moved), cotton porter, deal porter, dock warehouse porter, fish porter, grain porter, marine porter (carried luggage between train and ship), quay porter, quayside porter, riverside porter, sample porter, ship's porter, stone porter, timber porter, waterside porter, wine porter.

Rafter, raftsman; timber pondman (docks): a dock labourer who worked with timber rafts. The rafter would receive logs of pitch pine etc. from a ship or barge, these would then be made into rafts, by means of staples and chains, to be towed to timber pond in dock for storage.

Rail gangwayman: adjusted, and made secure, a railed gangway, from ship to pier or quayside, for passage of trucks.

Railman (docks): stood near ship rail during loading and unloading operations and signalled to **winchman** when to raise or lower goods.

Rigger, ship rigger (for working cargo): a specially skilled dock worker employed by master stevedores to rig up wire splicing, derricks, deck hoppers, chutes and other gear for loading and unloading ships. Riggers would also dismantle derricks, etc., when loading or unloading was completed.

Rope runner (colliery wharf): under the supervision of a colliery wharf foreman, rope runner was engaged in hauling trucks to and from coal twists and wharves during loading of ships with coal for export or carriage coastwise.

Runner, runnerman: *see* **carrier**. Sometimes further designated e.g. corn runner, fish runner.

Salt heaver: a dock labourer who shovelled salt from the hold of a ship into tubs for hoisting by crane or filled tubs on land for loading.

Shedman: a dock labourer engaged in sheds of docks or harbours.

Ship's discharger: *see* **unloader**.

Shootman: *see* **teemer**.

Slate picker (quay): a dock labourer engaged on a slate quay who sorted whole from broken slates.

Slate unloader (quay): a dock labourer specializing in carrying slates.

Slicer: a dock labourer who separated, with a wooden slice, bags of nitrate of soda that had stuck together during a voyage.

145

Stevedore, stower, ship stower: a loader that was specially skilled in stowing cargo in a ship's hold and was responsible to a master stevedore for proper stowing of cargo. Stevedores would ensure that goods were not too tightly packed, that they did not shift during a voyage, and that casks (and other containers liable to burst or leak) were not placed were they could damage other cargoes. A stevedore often directed a **holdsman** and assisted them in stowing cargoes.

Stocker (steamship): a dock labourer who loaded food supplies on a steamship for a victualling superintendent.

Sub-ganger (docks): a working foreman, who took charge, under instructions and general supervision, of a ganger or gang of dock labourers.

Teamer, coal (staithes): in charge of horses which were used to draw trucks of coal under cranes and into tipping sheds.

Teemer: one of a gang of dock labourers engaged in loading any kind of cargo that was shipped in bulk, from hoists or buckets. A coal teemer would stand on table of coal hoist on to which wagon was run; at a given signal, he would withdraw bolts from the hinged front or side of a wagon, which was then mechanically tilted, causing coal to fall down chute into ship's bunkers.

Timber pondman (docks): *see* **rafter**.

Tipper: carried or wheeled goods such as coal, gravel, sand and chalk to the quayside and tipped them down a chute into the hold of ship lying alongside quay.

Trapper (staithes), trap lad: (Tyneside terms) checked flow of coal from chute to ship's bunkers, by moving a lever which raised the end of the chute, to prevent coal being broken up too small by falling too heavily, or to prevent one part of bunker being heaped up too high.

Trimmer, coal: stood in ship's hold or bunker when being loaded with coal as cargo or as bunker coal; as each wagon was emptied down the chute into the hold by a **coal tipper**; trimmed (levelled) coal with shovel, so that it lay smooth and would not shift during a voyage, causing ship to list; signalled to tipper when ready to receive fresh load.

Trimmer, grain: 'trimmed' grain with shovel in ship's hold, so that it could be easily unloaded by grain suction apparatus; during loading, spread rain with shovels evenly in ship's hold, round stanchions, etc.

Unloader, coal: filled baskets, or other receptacles, with coal in ship's hold, and fastened them to rope or chain ready for hoisting to quayside. *See* **coal whipper**.

Unloader, dockside unloader; ship's discharger: a dock labourer principally engaged in unloading cargoes.

Wagonman, wagon rider; bank rider, brakesman (coal drops): accompanied loaded coal wagon (running alongside wagon or hanging on by hand) down gradient along which wagon descended by gravitation; dropped brake bar to check speed when necessary; at incline bottom, sometimes pulled-over point lever to allow wagon to run into coal hoist sidings.

Waterside baler: a dock labourer specially engaged in the handling and repacking of bales of wool or other baled goods at the waterside.

Whipper, coal: unloaded coal, with help of jib-hoist (crane fitted with receptacle for coal), from vessels into barge, lighter or railway wagon alongside; pulled levers to lower and raise receptacle to and from ship's hold for filling, etc.; at given signal from **trimmer**, swung filled receptacle into position and discharged coal there from into barge, lighter, or wagon.

Winchman: a **donkeyman** who controlled winches, under direction of an engineer.

Wing man, coal wing man: a **coal trimmer** who trimmed coal in ship's hold round stanchions.

INDEX